Financial Self-Assessment
a workbook for colleges

Nathan Dickmeyer   K. Scott Hughes

National Association of College and University Business Officers

Library of Congress Catalog Card Number:
80-83834

ISBN 0-915164-11-6

**Copyright © 1980 by the National Association of
College and University Business Officers
One Dupont Circle
Washington, D.C. 20036**

All rights reserved

Printed in the United States of America

Edited and designed by David W. Jacobson

Second Printing—August 1982

Contents

Foreword v

Acknowledgments vii

Introduction ix

1   Basis for Assessing Financial Condition   1
2   How to Use the Workbook   5
3   User Data   8
4   Calculation Worksheets   13
- Financial Resources   14
- Flexibility   22
- Nonfinancial Resources   30
- Changes Affecting Financial Resources   45

Appendix A   Self-Assessment Indicators and Calculations   62

Appendix B   Glossary   66

Appendix C   Retention of Entering Freshmen   68

Appendix D   Development and Testing of the Workbook   72

Foreword

This workbook was developed over a period of more than two years. During this period a preliminary edition was prepared and tested. The results were carefully reviewed and had a strong influence on the present volume.

There is an increasing interest in and need for financial indicators, especially within the institution but also among persons and agencies outside. It is hoped that this workbook will help to promote greater use of such indicators. Generally, data required for the calculations are readily available, which makes this workbook particularly easy to use.

In addition to the authors, many persons are responsible for the book; their names are listed in the acknowledgments. Readers are reminded that books published by NACUBO represent the association's position, unless otherwise indicated, even if authors' names are listed. All books undergo extensive review to insure that they are authoritative and that they reflect a consensus of the membership.

D. F. Finn
Executive Vice President
NACUBO

Acknowledgments

This project would not have been possible without the many contributions of the workbook task force, which nurtured the workbook idea and supervised and shaped the project. The following, who have all been financial consultants to colleges and universities, were members of the task force: Thomas O. James (chairperson), Birmingham Southern College; James W. Bryant, The Robert R. Moton Institute, Inc.; Douglas J. Collier, National Center for Higher Education Management Systems; William T. Haywood, Skidmore College; James R. Jordan, American Council on Education; B.A. Little, Moton Management Improvement Program; Robert W. Meyer, Ohio Wesleyan University; W. John Minter, John Minter Associates; Charles C. Teamer, Dillard University; Wayne M. Wormley, Fisk University; and Marwin O. Wrolstad, Lawrence University.

Salvatore B. Corrallo, of the U.S. Department of Education, supported the workbook idea as one that higher education would find interesting and useful.

Special thanks go to John Minter, who provided valuable comparative data and offered significant insights. His energetic involvement in the project shortened the time needed to complete it. Richard B. Jungkuntz, provost of Pacific Lutheran University, contributed an important technique for evaluating retention.

The manual serves as a model of interassociation cooperation. Joining in the effort were the National Association of College and University Business Officers (NACUBO) and the American Council on Education (ACE). M.J. Williams, staff to NACUBO's Programs for Small Colleges Committee, and Thomas James, chairperson of that committee (and of the workbook task force, as mentioned above), continually urged creation of the workbook, guided the effort, and actively assisted in workshops that used it. Laurel Radow, of NACUBO, was the project coordinator.

In addition to Dr. James, the members of the Programs for Small Colleges Committee were: Paul J. Aslanian, Macalester College; John H. Clark, California Institute of the Arts; Judith Cooper Guido, Union Theological Seminary; Rudolph E. Koletic, University of Tampa; Richard S. Thomas, Arkansas College; and Karl J. Warming, Berea College. The NACUBO Board of Directors charged this committee with general oversight of the project.

Particular thanks are extended to those who held discussions of drafts of the book. Ernest Bartell, now with Notre Dame University and formerly of the Association of Catholic Colleges and Universities, organized a meeting for Catholic institutions; Garry J. DeRose, president, did so for Colleges of Mid-America, Inc. Three task force members, Robert Meyer, Wayne Wormley, and Marwin Wrolstad, held similar discussions that allowed personnel from 40 institutions to fill out the workbook and review its contents. The result of these meetings was a shorter, more precise book.

The EXXON Education Foundation, which has consistently supported ideas of value to higher education, provided funds to bring the project to a successful conclusion. Robert L. Payton, Walter J. Kenworthy, and Richard R. Johnson, of the Foundation, helped to advance the project. Their continuing interest in management-related problems is appreciated. The National Center for Education Statistics funded a preliminary edition of the book.

About the authors: Nathan Dickmeyer is director of the Financial Conditions Project of the American Council on Education. K. Scott Hughes was director of NACUBO's Financial Management Center during the first half of the project and senior consultant with Peat, Marwick, Mitchell & Co. during the second half.

Introduction

This workbook can be used by members of governing boards, presidents, business officers, and other administrators of colleges and universities. Developed by NACUBO and ACE at a time when many institutions are facing difficult financial decisions, the workbook is intended to assist administrators in understanding and assessing the financial strengths and weaknesses of their institutions. It should be especially useful to independent colleges.

Need for Financial Assessment

Virtually all institutions of higher education have been affected by the spiraling costs of energy, plant construction, library books, and most services. Also creating pressure are the current and potential decline in the number of students of traditional college-going age, the maturing of buildings and faculty added during the expansion years, and the increase in regulatory requirements.

The nature and extent of these financial pressures must be examined so that appropriate strategies and policies can be developed. The analysis in this workbook provides the basis for determining courses of action that can help to assure institutional survival and health. In most cases, such actions consist of allocating scarce resources among the following:

- Working capital
- Endowment
- New fund-raising programs
- Faculty salaries
- Building repair
- Staff salaries
- Student recruitment
- New personnel
- Student retention
- Building construction
- Student scholarships

Allocations are, in effect, investments. An institution's optimal financial strategy, consisting of a carefully selected set of allocations, will offer the best "payoff" at the lowest risk. However, the payoff cannot be measured in simple monetary terms as it might be in the business world. It must be measured in terms of the institution's improved ability to meet its broad goals.

The ultimate objective of the workbook, as described more thoroughly in chapter 1, "Basis for Assessing Financial Condition," is to help those using it to evaluate the college's financial condition relative to its financial risks. These financial risks depend on external factors such as demographic changes or the general economy and on the college's revenue and expenditure structure. For example, a college highly dependent on grant and contract revenues may face relatively high risk, as may an institution with a comparatively high proportion of fixed costs.

The workbook does not remove the "art" from "the art of administration." There is much about institutions that cannot be quantified: leadership, morale, community spirit, and legend, for example. Also, there is little about the future that can be foretold. The workbook enables users to calculate a number of statistics that are necessary for assessing institutional risks and resources. These computed statistics are indicators that form the basis for assembling the institution's financial strategies.

Need for the Workbook Approach

A simplified workbook approach to financial assessment has been one of the major developments of this project. This approach encourages administrators to systematically examine the financial condition of their colleges with a tested and specified set of data-gathering and computational steps.

The workbook approach also explains the relationships among the statistics and how those relationships can be used to develop a financial profile.

The workbook contains median values that allow statistical comparisons among institutions. These data, provided by John Minter Associates, are from Liberal Arts Colleges II.* Business officers may wish to negotiate directly with John Minter Associates to obtain more specific comparative statistics based on a particular set of peer institutions such as those that are denomination-affiliated, that are located within specific geographic areas, or that have the same enrollment size.

Organization of the Workbook

The workbook has been organized so the user can read enough material to gain an understanding of the basic concepts of college finances without having to perform the statistical calculations and analysis. The material in chapter 1 describes the basis for assessing institutional strategies. Chapter 2 describes data sources within the institution and procedures to be used in the financial self-assessment. Chapter 3 consists of worksheets to be used for recording data from institutional sources. These data are the basis of the calculations in the workbook.

Chapter 4, the bulk of the book, contains worksheets for calculating statistics in four key categories that affect the college's financial condition. Each worksheet covers one statistic and includes a discussion of the statistic's significance, median values for similar institutions, explanation of the calculations, interpretations of the statistic, limitations of the statistic, and suggestions for further analysis.

*See Glossary.

1 Basis for Assessing Financial Condition

The theory underlying the assessment of a college's financial condition is embedded in a larger view of the operations and strategies of the college. The analyst must be aware of the college's purposes, academic programs, and management philosophy.

Institutional Strategies

In this discussion a strategy is a long-range plan of action that is intertwined with the mission, goals, policies, plans, and budgets of the college. Many strategies are in operation at any one time, and administrators need to understand how current ones contribute to the college's successful operation.

Strategies can be grouped into four broad areas: academic program, marketing, management and control, and finance. The list below illustrates some of the functions within each area.

Sample Institutional Management Strategy Areas

Academic
- ☐ Mission
- ☐ Academic program
- ☐ Faculty policies
- ☐ Research policies
- ☐ Admissions policies

Management and Control
- ☐ Purchasing
- ☐ Personnel
- ☐ Cash management
- ☐ Investments
- ☐ Professional development
- ☐ Property management

Marketing
- ☐ Fund raising
- ☐ Public relations
- ☐ Media
- ☐ Alumni association
- ☐ Recruitment

Financial
- ☐ Revenue mix
- ☐ Resource mix
- ☐ Expenditure mix
- ☐ Risk position

Statistics in the workbook can be used to monitor changes in revenue mix, expenditure mix, resource mix, and risk position. A major consideration in building the college's financial strategy is the balance between risks and resources. As risk increases (for example, with a drop in applications), resources must increase (for example, from reserve funds) if the institution is to be protected from the full trauma of revenue fluctuations.

Strategies must maximize revenue performance without unduly increasing risk. Strategies must also match expenditure patterns with overall college goals. The statistics in the workbook are designed to assist in the evaluation of current strategies and the planning of new ones.

Financial performance is greatly affected by the success of strategies in other areas. Thus, financial analysis requires at least a partial assessment of nonfinancial strategies that cover, for example, retention, admissions, and building maintenance. The workbook ties together the assessment of many types of strategies.

Framework for Understanding Financial Statistics

An institution's financial condition depends on two closely related factors: its basic financial structure and the environment. Changes in the environment, such as inflation and declining applications, can affect the institution's financial stability and structure. Also, changes in financial structure, such as increased emphasis on academics, can affect the environment and cause a change in the type of student who applies.

Coupled with the concept of financial *condition* is the concept of financial *risk*. The ease with which an institution's financial stability is affected by the environment is referred to as its *relative financial risk*. The more susceptible an institution is to the negative effects of the environment, the greater is its financial risk.

The assessment of financial condition and relative financial risk relies on the evaluation of structured sets of statistics in four categories:

- Financial resources
- Flexibility
- Nonfinancial resources
- Changes affecting financial resources

Financial Resources

Accumulated resources are as important to a college as they are to a profit-making organization. Relative financial wealth gives an organization the ability to seek opportunities, handle unexpected financial disruptions, and minimize the risk of severe retrenchment.

A financially sound college will have enough financial resources to meet its immediate commitments such as salaries, other operating expenses, and debt service. It will also have a capital base (i.e., endowment and reserves) sufficient to provide a financial cushion as well as offer a stabilizing influence on the flow of revenues.

The three statistics used to assess the college's financial resources are separated by time phase (short-, intermediate-, and long-term). Two additional statistics in this section reflect "Hidden Financial Resources" and have been included to bring into the analysis such factors as land sales, potential donations, and wealth of affiliated organizations. These items are not normally documented in the college's financial statements, yet they can have a material effect on an assessment of available financial resources. Appendix A lists all statistics used in the workbook.

In site-visit tests of the workbook, a statistic helpful as a quick summary of overall financial condition was the **Available Funds Ratio**, which assesses intermediate-term financial resources. It combines the unrestricted current fund balance and quasi-endowment market value, showing this sum as a proportion of educational and general expenditures plus mandatory transfers. The statistic reflects the institution's ability to match expenditures with revenues over time and measures the amount of reserves available for unforeseen financial difficulties or new opportunities.

Flexibility

Maintaining the flexibility of the institution is important for minimizing the risks of revenue loss or budget misalignment. The greater the institution's financial inflexibility, the greater the need for financial resources to protect and buffer core activities, such as the academic program, from debilitating fluctuations in revenues and costs.

The **Debt Service to Revenue Ratio** measures the amount of revenue not available for the buildup of other resources; the **Acceptance Rate** measures the flexibility to accept a higher percentage of the applicant pool; and the **Tenured Faculty Ratio** measures the administration's freedom to make budget changes by altering the size of the teaching staff.

The site visits have shown the **Acceptance Rate** to be very significant. If this statistic has a high value, the institution's applicant pool is probably limited, and there is a good possibility that continued decline in the number of students of traditional college age will have an adverse effect on the college. However, if the statistic has a low value, the college probably has some flexibility in its admissions program and may experience a relatively minor negative effect from such a decline.

Nonfinancial Resources

The assessment of nonfinancial resources can reveal significant changes that cannot be identified by standard financial analyses. Some financial strategies sustain what appears to be a financially sound organization. However, this appearance may have been achieved through neglect of areas such as academic programs, student services, physical facilities, or faculty.

The nonfinancial resources examined in this assessment are students, institutional attraction, academic programs, faculty, staff, and physical plant.

The most informative statistic in this category may be the **Instruction Proportion**. A decrease in the portion of a college's budget allotted to instruction may be caused by factors such as rising administrative support costs, high fixed costs such as debt payments and utilities, or growing scholarship programs. A decrease in the **Instruction Proportion** may signify a material change in the college's priorities for resource allocation.

Changes Affecting Financial Resources

The statistics in this section gauge the institution's ability to sustain a balanced stream of revenues and expenditures. They also demonstrate significant revenue and expenditure flow changes that may affect financial condition.

The most informative statistics may be the **Student-Derived Revenue Trends** and the **Proportion of Revenue from Gifts.**

Overall Assessment of Financial Condition

The workbook should ultimately lead to a summary of the institution's financial condition. The summary should include answers to the following questions:

1. What have been the major external factors affecting the college's financial condition?

The search for an answer to this question must begin in the "Changes Affecting Financial Resources" section, where enrollment trends, the effect of inflation on costs per student, inflation erosion of tuition revenue, and gift assistance are measured. Enrollment as measured by financial full-time equivalent students appears to be the single most important external factor, based on the project's site-visit evaluations.

2. What have been the major administrative policies affecting the college's financial condition?

These may not be easily recognized. Many of the workbook statistics monitor important, though perhaps unwritten, policies that currently guide the institution. These policies include:

□ The allocation of resources to reserves, monitored by the **Available Funds Ratio.**
□ The allocation of resources to academic programs, monitored by the **Instruction Proportion.**
□ The allocation of resources to student recruitment and retention, monitored by the **Institutional Attraction Statistics.**
□ The allocation of resources to physical facilities, monitored by the **Deferred Maintenance Ratio.**
□ The allocation of resources to faculty and staff, monitored by (1) **Change in Average Faculty Compensation** and (2) **Students to Adminstrative Exempt Staff.**
□ The effort to minimize risk exposure, as measured by the flexibility ratios **(Debt Service to Revenue Ratio, Acceptance Rate, and Tenured Faculty Ratio).**
□ The investment in future effort relative to current effort, as monitored by trends in the **Endowment Ratio** and in the resource allocations mentioned above.
□ The financing strategy of the institution, as measured by changes in the institution's dependence on tuition and gift revenues.

3. How have the institution's financial resources been affected by external factors and administrative policies?

This question may be answered with an examination of trends in the statistics in the "Financial Resources" section. Sound financial condition requires liquid assets to pay expenses on time, reserves to protect the institution from unfavorable contingencies, and sufficient capital resources to provide both the symbol and the reality of extra support for programs beyond the tuition normally provided by students.

4. How has the institution's financial risk position changed in relation to the institution's financial resources?

To answer this question, changes in the financial reserves of the institution, as measured by the **Available Funds Ratio,** must be compared to trends in the institution's flexibility. If the **Debt Service to Revenue Ratio,** the **Acceptance Rate,** or the **Tenured Faculty Ratio** has increased, the institution should reexamine its policies for building financial reserves. The greater the inflexibility, the greater the need for financial resources.

5. What changes have occurred in nonfinancial resources that may have had an effect on the institution's financial resources?

Even if the workbook demonstrates in answer to question 4 that the institution has successfully built up financial resources, that increase may have occurred at the expense of nonfinancial resources. A comparison of trends in the "Financial Resources" and "Nonfinancial Resources" sections will help to answer this question of balance among institutional resources. Financial reserves may grow at a time when faculty salaries, building maintenance, or institutional attraction shrinks.

6. What is the institution's overall financial condition?

At this point science stops, and the art of assessment begins. After completing the workbook, the analyst may see many possible courses of action, some running counter to conventional wisdom about the prosperity of the institution. The art of assessment involves blending these perceptions and potential courses of action into a coherent picture of the college's condition. Discussion of past and future financial strategies should flow from the assessment, as should judgments about which aspects of the assessment are most important to each institution and what may be missing from the analysis.

The workbook's Core Statistics should be examined first. These are "special alert" statistics that can highlight the most damaging or encouraging financial trends in the institution.

The Core Statistics are:

- **Available Funds Ratio**
- **Acceptance Rate**
- **Academic Program: Instruction Proportion, Instruction per FTE Student**
- **Faculty: Change in Average Compensation, Student to Faculty Ratio**
- **Student-Derived Revenue Trends: Constant (1971) Dollar Net Student Revenue, Constant (1971) Dollar Tuition Rate, Financial FTE Enrollments, Tuition Discount Factor.**

An institution's decisions on the relative importance of various statistics should be based on that institution's mission and special situation. For example, institutions with strong community or religious support may find that financial resource measures or factors are not as critical as other types of resource measures. The pattern of strengths and weaknesses that differentiates the institution from its peers is crucial to determining the relative importance of assessment factors.

Further analysis or special sensitivity may be needed to complete the broad assessment. Although a statistic may show falling relative faculty salaries, for example, the decline may be caused by recruitment of young faculty and retirements. Discovery of subtle or concealed factors behind the trends is necessary for determining the real meaning of many of the statistics.

As the potential for enrollment decline forces new priorities on many institutions, the need for financial reserves, strong retention, competitive academic programs, and well-maintained physical facilities is increasing. For most institutions the statistics that monitor these factors will provide the core for an overall assessment. Other institutions in other circumstances may focus on different statistics measuring different factors.

2 How to Use the Workbook

The workbook has been designed so that financial officers, in cooperation with the registrar and admissions officers, will be best equipped to fill it out. Specialized language has been eliminated as much as possible.

Identification of Institutional Data

The workbook allows a logical presentation of many types of data. The "User Data" worksheet in chapter 3 lists all institutional data categories needed for the assessment and has spaces for recording information for each of seven years (1976-1982).

The key institutional data sources are:

- Annual financial reports: Statement of revenues, expenditures, and other changes; balance sheet
- Annual student aid reports
- AAUP salary survey results (or equivalent)
- Annual personnel statistics
- Annual reports of the admissions officer
- Annual reports of the registrar

In addition to the above, a number of supplemental reports or estimates are necessary. To complete the workbook, for example, the amount of deferred plant maintenance at the end of each fiscal year will have to be estimated.

Data for five consecutive fiscal years, FY76 through FY80, will be needed to calculate the statistics. Because self-assessment emphasizes trend analysis, those using the workbook should be certain that information for each item on the User Data worksheet in chapter 3 is as consistent from year to year as possible. This insures that users will see accurate trends. Information from the worksheet is transferred as needed to the Calculation Worksheets in chapter 4.

Dates on all worksheets run to 1982 to allow annual updating of the workbook. No projections are to be made, except where specifically indicated.

A comprehensive glossary is provided in appendix B. It is intended to encourage the use of consistent terminology and classification structures and is based on materials developed by the following national organizations:

- American Association of Collegiate Registrars and Admissions Officers
- National Association of College and University Business Officers
- National Center for Higher Education Management Systems

Filling Out the Workbook

In order to facilitate completion of the workbook, the following steps are suggested:

1. Read through the workbook to gain an understanding of its approach and style.
2. Gather the key data sources referred to above that contain the data used for the analysis. The reports should be for the five most recent fiscal years.
3. Photocopy the User Data worksheet (pp. 8-12) and on the copy fill in all data.
4. Starting with the Core Statistics, proceed through the workbook, inserting data on the Calculation Worksheets by referring to the User Data worksheet as required. Calculate all statistics.
5. Starting with the Core Statistics, evaluate the significance of each statistic.
6. When all statistics have been interpreted, develop an overall analysis describing the institution's financial condition.
7. Prepare reports that illustrate findings of the analysis and that are tailored to the needs of appropriate decision makers (trustees, president, etc.).

The workbook can and should be molded to fit the needs of each institution. After using the workbook for the first time, administrators can add their own statistics for calculation or make other adjustments.

Preparation of Reports

College officials may wish to prepare annual financial assessments. These reports are useful at the start of each academic year and may be presented to the governing board in the fall, as well as to faculty, students, and other interested parties. The assessments will provide important background material as officials begin constructing the subsequent year's operating budget.

The following outline illustrates how the statistics in the workbook can form the basis of reports on financial condition. Such reports should include only those topics and statistics that are relevant to the institution's situation and that may help administrators to formulate courses of action.

Some of the material in the outline is explained in *Financial Responsibilities of Governing Boards of Colleges and Universities*, a NACUBO/AGB* book. *A Planning Manual for Colleges* and *A Management Reporting Manual for Colleges*, published by NACUBO, also describe the use of financial information in the development of college plans and are sources of additional information.

*Association of Governing Boards of Universities and Colleges

Outline of Sample Report

Introduction

Purpose of the report
- ☐ Assessment of financial condition
- ☐ Background material for review of administrative policies and for preparation of budget

Scope of report
- ☐ Five-year historical analysis
- ☐ Financial assessment
- ☐ Use of comparative statistical data

Audience
- ☐ President and executive staff
- ☐ Faculty and student governing bodies
- ☐ Governing board

Approach to the analysis
- ☐ Use of the workbook
- ☐ Description of relative financial risk and financial flexibility

Summary of Observations

Relative financial risk condition
- ☐ Identification of major financial strengths and weaknesses

Relative flexibility
- ☐ Identification of options available to improve financial position

External Factors Affecting Financial Condition
- ☐ Enrollment trends (pp. 28-29)
- ☐ Inflation (pp. 38-39, 57-58)
- ☐ Local economic conditions
- ☐ National student test scores (pp. 30-33)

Administrative Policies Affecting Financial Condition
- ☐ Resource allocations (pp. 57-58)
- ☐ Salary levels (pp. 38-39)
- ☐ Tenure (pp. 26-27)
- ☐ Use of part-time faculty
- ☐ Admissions (pp. 24-25, 30-33)
- ☐ Student aid
- ☐ Academic program offerings
- ☐ Student-faculty ratios (pp. 38-39)

Financial Resources
- ☐ Unrestricted current fund position (pp. 14-15)
- ☐ Available fund position (pp. 16-17)
- ☐ Endowment position (pp. 18-19)
- ☐ Hidden financial resources (pp. 20-21)

Flexibility
- ☐ Debt service burden (pp. 22-23)
- ☐ Acceptance rate (pp. 24-25)
- ☐ Tenure ratio (pp. 26-27)
- ☐ Hidden financial risks (pp. 28-29)

Nonfinancial Resources
- ☐ Students (pp. 30-33)
- ☐ Institutional attraction (pp. 34-35)
- ☐ Academic program (pp. 36-37)
- ☐ Faculty (pp. 38-39)
- ☐ Staff (pp. 40-41)
- ☐ Physical plant (pp. 42-43)
- ☐ Hidden nonfinancial resources (p. 44)

Revenues and Expenditures
- ☐ Revenues by source (pp. 50-52)
- ☐ Expenditures by object and function (pp. 59-61)

Causal Relationships
- ☐ Changes in external factors compared to changes in flexibility, financial resources, and financial inflows and outflows
- ☐ Flexibility compared to financial resources
- ☐ Changes in nonfinancial resources compared to changes in financial resources
- ☐ Changes in administrative policies compared to changes in financial resources

Recommendations for Strategies
- ☐ Continuations
- ☐ New strategies

Charts and Graphs
- ☐ Enrollment trends
- ☐ Student-faculty ratio
- ☐ Retention
- ☐ Salary trends compared to inflation
- ☐ Ratio of matriculations to applications
- ☐ Ratio of instruction to operating budgets
- ☐ Ratio of expenditures to revenues

3 User Data

Instructions and Information

1. Use this worksheet to compile all institutional data for calculation of the statistics in chapter 4. To permit ready reference, photocopy this worksheet and place all figures on the duplicate copy.

2. Each item on this worksheet is discrete.

3. Information for each item should be consistent from year to year.

4. Information from this worksheet is to be transferred, as needed, directly to the Calculation Worksheets in chapter 4.

5. All dates here and on the Calculation Worksheets run to 1982 to allow annual updating of the workbook. Do not make projections, except where indicated.

6. Asterisks on this worksheet indicate data needed for calculation of Core Statistics.

	Fiscal Year Ending:						
Revenues (from statement of revenues and expenditures)	1976	1977	1978	1979	1980	1981	1982
*1. Tuition and fees ($000)	$_____	$_____	$_____	$_____	$_____	$_____	$_____
2. Government appropriations (federal, state, and local) ($000)	$_____	$_____	$_____	$_____	$_____	$_____	$_____
3. Government grants and contracts (federal, state, and local, including scholarship aid, SEOGs, work-study revenues, research funds, education "title" funds, etc.) ($000)	$_____	$_____	$_____	$_____	$_____	$_____	$_____
4. Private gifts, grants, and contracts (include unrestricted *and* restricted) ($000)	$_____	$_____	$_____	$_____	$_____	$_____	$_____
5. Endowment income (include unrestricted *and* restricted) ($000)	$_____	$_____	$_____	$_____	$_____	$_____	$_____
6. Other current fund revenues ($000)	$_____	$_____	$_____	$_____	$_____	$_____	$_____
7. Auxiliary enterprise revenue ($000)	$_____	$_____	$_____	$_____	$_____	$_____	$_____
8. Revenue from independent operations ($000)	$_____	$_____	$_____	$_____	$_____	$_____	$_____
9. Current fund revenues (include unrestricted *and* restricted) (add items 1 through 8) ($000)	$_____	$_____	$_____	$_____	$_____	$_____	$_____
10. Value of contributed services (even if included above) ($000)	$_____	$_____	$_____	$_____	$_____	$_____	$_____
11. Financial support from affiliated organizations or patron foundations (even if included above) ($000)	$_____	$_____	$_____	$_____	$_____	$_____	$_____
*12. Tuition and fee rate per year for a full-time student ($000)	$_____	$_____	$_____	$_____	$_____	$_____	$_____

*Data needed for Core Statistics.

Fiscal Year Ending:

Expenditures and Transfers (from statement of revenues and expenditures)	1976	1977	1978	1979	1980	1981	1982
*13. Instruction ($000)	$_____	$_____	$_____	$_____	$_____	$_____	$_____
14. Research ($000)	$_____	$_____	$_____	$_____	$_____	$_____	$_____
15. Public service ($000)	$_____	$_____	$_____	$_____	$_____	$_____	$_____
16. Academic support ($000)	$_____	$_____	$_____	$_____	$_____	$_____	$_____
17. Student services ($000)	$_____	$_____	$_____	$_____	$_____	$_____	$_____
18. Institutional support ($000)	$_____	$_____	$_____	$_____	$_____	$_____	$_____
19. Operation and maintenance of plant ($000)	$_____	$_____	$_____	$_____	$_____	$_____	$_____
*20. Scholarships and fellowships from unrestricted funds ($000)	$_____	$_____	$_____	$_____	$_____	$_____	$_____
*21. Scholarships and fellowships from restricted funds ($000)	$_____	$_____	$_____	$_____	$_____	$_____	$_____
*22. Mandatory transfers ($000)	$_____	$_____	$_____	$_____	$_____	$_____	$_____
*23. Educational & general expenditures plus mandatory transfers ($000) (E&G + MT) (add items 13 through 22)	$_____	$_____	$_____	$_____	$_____	$_____	$_____
24. Utilities included in operation and maintenance of plant (electricity, gas, coal, steam, water, etc.) (see item 19) ($000)	$_____	$_____	$_____	$_____	$_____	$_____	$_____
*25. Average full-time faculty compensation (salary and benefits) ($000)	$_____	$_____	$_____	$_____	$_____	$_____	$_____
26. Average exempt staff salaries (administrative and institutional services) ($000)	$_____	$_____	$_____	$_____	$_____	$_____	$_____
27. Debt service due for all funds (within the fiscal year listed) ($000)	$_____	$_____	$_____	$_____	$_____	$_____	$_____
28. Total books and periodicals expenditures ($000)	$_____	$_____	$_____	$_____	$_____	$_____	$_____

*Data needed for Core Statistics.

Fiscal Year Ending:

	1976	1977	1978	1979	1980	1981	1982

Balance Sheet Items

29. Unrestricted current fund assets ($000) $_____ $_____ $_____ $_____ $_____ $_____ $_____

30. Student accounts receivable at end of fiscal year (not including credit balances or advance billings) ($000) $_____ $_____ $_____ $_____ $_____ $_____ $_____

31. Uncollectible student accounts written off in fiscal year ($000) $_____ $_____ $_____ $_____ $_____ $_____ $_____

32. Unrestricted current fund liabilities ($000) $_____ $_____ $_____ $_____ $_____ $_____ $_____

*33. Unrestricted current fund balance (should equal item 29 minus item 32) ($000) $_____ $_____ $_____ $_____ $_____ $_____ $_____

*34. Quasi-endowment market value ($000) $_____ $_____ $_____ $_____ $_____ $_____ $_____

35. Endowment (including quasi) market value ($000) $_____ $_____ $_____ $_____ $_____ $_____ $_____

36. Value of marketable land (not included in endowment) ($000) $_____ $_____ $_____ $_____ $_____ $_____ $_____

Deferred Maintenance

37. Estimate of deferred physical plant maintenance ($000) $_____ $_____ $_____ $_____ $_____ $_____ $_____

Personnel

38. Number of tenured faculty or faculty with long-term contracts (greater than five years) _____ _____ _____ _____ _____ _____ _____

*39. FTE (full-time equivalent) faculty (fall) _____ _____ _____ _____ _____ _____ _____

40. FTE administrative exempt staff (excluding auxiliary staff) (fall) _____ _____ _____ _____ _____ _____ _____

*Data needed for Core Statistics.

Students (from admissions reports)
(Note: Items 41-49 require information from **academic year**, not fiscal year.)

Fiscal Year Ending:

	1976	1977	1978	1979	1980	1981	1982
41. Inquiries (bona fide, not from purchased lists)	_____	_____	_____	_____	_____	_____	_____
*42. Freshmen applications	_____	_____	_____	_____	_____	_____	_____
*43. Transfer applications	_____	_____	_____	_____	_____	_____	_____
*44. Acceptances of freshmen and transfer applicants	_____	_____	_____	_____	_____	_____	_____
45. New students (freshmen and transfers)	_____	_____	_____	_____	_____	_____	_____
46. Percentage of previous year's eligible students who enroll for next class	____%	____%	____%	____%	____%	____%	____%
47. Average test scores of entering freshmen	_____	_____	_____	_____	_____	_____	_____
48. Percentage of entering students from top 20% of high school class	____%	____%	____%	____%	____%	____%	____%
49. Percentage of entering students from top 40% of high school class	____%	____%	____%	____%	____%	____%	____%
*50. FTE students (fall)	_____	_____	_____	_____	_____	_____	_____
51. Total student headcount (fall)	_____	_____	_____	_____	_____	_____	_____

Financial Aid (from financial aid office reports)

	1976	1977	1978	1979	1980	1981	1982
52. Amount of BEOGs *not included* in items 20 through 22 ($000)	$_____	$_____	$_____	$_____	$_____	$_____	$_____
53. State student aid *not included* in items 20 through 22 ($000)	$_____	$_____	$_____	$_____	$_____	$_____	$_____
54. Federal work-study *not included* in items 20 through 22 ($000)	$_____	$_____	$_____	$_____	$_____	$_____	$_____
55. Other government student aid *not included* in items 20 through 22 ($000)	$_____	$_____	$_____	$_____	$_____	$_____	$_____
56. All government student aid *not included* in revenues (items 20 through 22) (add items 52 through 55) ($000)	$_____	$_____	$_____	$_____	$_____	$_____	$_____

Projected Data

	1981	1982	1983	1984	1985
57. Potential *first-time* student enrollment decline (% decline from base year 1980 because of changing demographics)	____%	____%	____%	____%	____%

*Data needed for Core Statistics.

4 Calculation Worksheets

Instructions and Information
1. Write all figures directly on the following Calculation Worksheets. The completed workbook will thus be a comprehensive self-assessment document.
2. On all Calculation Worksheets the statistics that are most important for the financial analysis appear in **bold** type.
3. Worksheets containing Core Statistics are labeled with large **bold** headings.

Indicators for Financial Self-Assessment

Financial Resources
- Short-term—Unrestricted Current Fund Ratio
- Intermediate-term—Available Funds Ratio*
- Long-term—Endowment Ratio

Flexibility
- Debt Service to Revenue Ratio
- Acceptance Rate*
- Tenured Faculty Ratio

Nonfinancial Resources
- Student Characteristics
- Institutional Attraction
- Academic Program*
- Faculty*
- Staff
- Deferred Physical Plant Maintenance

Changes Affecting Financial Resources
- Student-Derived Revenue Trends*
- Government-Derived Inflow Proportion
- Revenue Bar Graphs
- Contributed Services
- Expenditures per Student
- Expenditures—Unit Trends
- Expenditure Bar Graphs

* Core Statistic

Financial Resources: Indicators and Calculations

A. Short-term—Unrestricted Current Fund Ratio

Calculation: $$\frac{\text{Unrestricted current fund assets}}{\text{Unrestricted current fund liabilities}}$$

B. Intermediate-term—Available Funds Ratio*

Calculation: $$\frac{\text{Unrestricted current fund balance plus quasi-endowment market value}}{\text{Educational and general expenditures plus mandatory transfers (E\&G + MT)}}$$

C. Long-term—Endowment Ratio

Calculation: $$\frac{\text{Endowment market value}}{\text{E\&G + MT}}$$

Hidden Financial Resources (estimated only):

D. Value of Marketable Land Ratio

Calculation: $$\frac{\text{Value of marketable land}}{\text{E\&G + MT}}$$

E. Financial Support from Affiliated Organizations or Patron Foundations

Calculation: $$\frac{\text{Financial support from affiliated organizations or patron foundations}}{\text{E\&G + MT}}$$

*Core Statistic

Category: **Financial Resources**
Selected Statistic:
Short-term—Unrestricted Current Fund Ratio

Significance of Statistic

This statistic is a ratio of unrestricted current fund assets to unrestricted current fund liabilities. The value of the ratio is an indication of funds available to pay currently owed liabilities. Current fund assets are usually regarded as the most liquid of the institution's financial resources and are used to pay current operating expenses. One of the main reasons for keeping this ratio safely above one and preferably above two is to provide adequate working capital. Bills can be paid on time, less time is spent borrowing funds, discounts can be taken, and interest on debt is minimized. These are signs of a well-run, financially healthy organization with minimal cash-flow problems.

Calculation Worksheet   Fiscal year ending:

			1976	1977	1978	1979	1980	1981	1982
A.	Unrestricted current fund assets	(29*)	$_____	$_____	$_____	$_____	$_____	$_____	$_____
B.	Unrestricted current fund liabilities	(32*)	$_____	$_____	$_____	$_____	$_____	$_____	$_____
C.	**Unrestricted Current Fund Ratio** (A divided by B):		_____	_____	_____	_____	_____	_____	_____

*Refers to corresponding item on worksheet in chapter 3, "User Data."

Median Values for Similar Institutions   FTE ≤ 1500, from Liberal Arts Colleges II

	1976	1977	1978	1979	1980	1981	1982
Unrestricted Current Fund Ratio (17 institutions)	1.167	.969	.870	1.193			

Source: Audited financial statements coded to NACUBO standards, John Minter Associates, Boulder, Colorado.

Explanation of Calculations

Current fund assets include cash, securities, accounts receivable, prepaid expenses, and inventories. Current fund assets may also include amounts loaned to other funds ("due from"). Current fund liabilities include accrued payroll, accounts payable, accrued revenue, notes payable, and money borrowed from other funds ("due to").

The ratio uses only unrestricted current fund assets and liabilities. While this may be conservative in that many assets of the restricted funds (such as gifts restricted to "academic programs") may be only loosely restricted, many restricted assets such as the cash from advance receipts of student financial aid can be used only for very specific purposes and cannot be used to pay unrestricted liabilities. Thus, restricted funds are excluded from this liquidity calculation.

Interpretations

Ratios above two. The institution probably has adequate unrestricted current fund assets to prevent immediate or short-term financial difficulty.

Ratios between one and two. The institution may wish to reevaluate its cash management policies. If most of the assets such as cash or marketable securities are liquid, and if many of the liabilities are not due immediately (for example, amounts due to other funds), then a lower ratio is probably acceptable. If no margin of safety is revealed in the cash management analysis, then business officers may need to increase assets and retire liabilities by budgeting surpluses through greater austerity. They may also wish to manage cash with a monthly cash-flow plan.

Ratios below one. Cash-flow difficulty is more probable. Unless the institution has other sizable reserves, difficulty with creditors is possible. The institution may have insufficient assets to cover debts, especially if it is borrowing heavily on a short-term basis. Careful and alert cash management may be necessary when cash reserves are almost depleted.

Limitations

Liquid assets may be available in other funds. Notably, the plant fund may have assets that are not committed to any current project. These assets may be available in an emergency and, at the discretion of the governing board, can be redirected to the current fund.

Further Analysis

If weakness is indicated in the institution's working capital position, the following analyses may be warranted.

The institution may wish to establish a cash-flow forecast, based on previous years' records, showing monthly revenues and expenditures for at least one year. Months with traditionally low balances can be highlighted. These months might then be targeted for early tuition payment drives or special fund-raising programs.

If the institution can use restricted assets such as reserves for payment of current fund debt, then the ratio should be calculated with these assets included.

An examination of restricted current fund liabilities occasionally reveals amounts such as refunds due that are owed to external agencies (for example, NDSL). To highlight potential cash-flow problems, it may be necessary to include in the calculation any liabilities of this nature and any restricted fund assets available to cover them.

Core Statistic

Category: **Financial Resources**
Selected Statistic:
Intermediate-term—Available Funds Ratio

Significance of Statistic

The unrestricted current fund balance and quasi-endowment represent the financial reserves of the institution. Unlike pure endowment, quasi-endowment funds can be used if the governing board is given adequate time to consider transferring them. These quasi-endowment reserves can help to diminish the adverse effect on current programs caused by revenue declines and unforeseen expenditure increases. They can also be used as venture capital for innovative educational ideas. Institutions that have not run consistent deficits are in generally good financial condition and have been able to sustain their financial reserves.

Calculation Worksheet

	Fiscal year ending:		1976	1977	1978	1979	1980	1981	1982
A.	Unrestricted current fund balance	(33*)	$_____	$_____	$_____	$_____	$_____	$_____	$_____
B.	Quasi-endowment market value	(34*)	$_____	$_____	$_____	$_____	$_____	$_____	$_____
C.	Available funds (add A and B)		$_____	$_____	$_____	$_____	$_____	$_____	$_____
D.	E&G + MT	(23*)	$_____	$_____	$_____	$_____	$_____	$_____	$_____
E.	**Available Funds Ratio (C divided by D):**		_____	_____	_____	_____	_____	_____	_____

*Refers to corresponding item on worksheet in chapter 3, "User Data."

Median Values for Similar Institutions

FTE ≤ 1500, from Liberal Arts Colleges II

	1976	1977	1978	1979	1980	1981	1982
Available Funds Ratio (using book value) (17 institutions)	.130	.157	.138	.080			

Source: Audited financial statements coded to NACUBO standards, John Minter Associates, Boulder, Colorado.

Explanation of Calculations

The fund balance for any fund is the difference between assets and liabilities. The fund balance is positive when assets are larger than liabilities and negative when liabilities exceed assets. In a year when revenues exceed expenditures, assets may increase accordingly, liabilities may decrease, or both may occur. In a year when expenditures exceed revenues, the extra costs of that year's operations must be funded by drawing on assets, if available, or by borrowing (i.e., increasing liabilities). In either case the deficit causes the fund balance to decline.

Because of their close relation, the unrestricted current fund balance and the quasi-endowment have been chosen here to comprise "available funds." Increases in quasi-endowment generally consist of transfers from the current fund. These transfers are made with the approval of the governing board and may result from an unusually large unrestricted gift or a current fund surplus. As previously stated, quasi-endowment funds may be withdrawn by board action.

Dividing the available funds by a year's educational and general expenditures plus mandatory transfers (E&G + MT) measures the size of the college's financial reserves. For example, a ratio of one-half would mean that the institution has sufficient financial reserves to continue operations for six months without revenue inflow.

If there are current fund balances that have been specifically designated as reserves, they should be included with the unrestricted current fund balance. Some institutions set aside portions of surpluses as operating reserves.

Interpretations

Comparison with peer institutions. The medians in the "Median Values for Similar Institutions" section above seem too low for safety, given the probability of enrollment decline, the increased tenuring of faculty, and the rising costs of energy. Determination of what constitutes "adequate" net available funds in reserve should be based on the analysis in the "Flexibility" section of this workbook. The internal flexibility assessment is a more accurate indicator of reserves than comparative assessment.

Declining ratios. A decline may be interpreted as a positive trend if the institution has chosen to invest its reserves in a new program or to fortify an existing one. In most cases, however, a decline in available funds means the institution is finding it increasingly difficult to balance revenues and expenditures. The college is probably incurring deficits, and its reserves are being diminished. On the other hand, if the institution has experienced enrollment growth, a decline in the ratio may indicate that reserves are failing to grow as fast as the institution's budget.

Increasing ratios. Institutions with an increasing ratio are better prepared for financial disruptions. Further analysis, however, is needed to confirm that other resources, including buildings, faculty, or students, are not being neglected. Analysis of these factors follows in the "Nonfinancial Resources" section.

Limitations

Some institutions may have hidden financial resources such as land or financially sound affiliated organizations that make the negative interpretation of low fund balances incorrect.

Also, some institutions may have reserves in other funds such as the plant fund that may offset low fund balances in the current and quasi-endowment funds. Because of the many possible restrictions on them, however, accumulated plant funds have not been included in the calculation of available funds.

Further Analysis

Should the ratio above demonstrate a decline in or a lack of reserves, and should no hidden resources mitigate this decline, an examination of the institution's marketing, control, and financial strategies is needed.

Category: **Financial Resources**
Selected Statistic:
   Long-term—Endowment Ratio

Significance of Statistic

This ratio compares the institution's endowment fund, including quasi-endowment, at market to the amount of yearly expenditures (E&G + MT). The endowment fund represents accumulated resources that provide income for extra service to students above what is "purchased" with tuition. Endowment income is an intrinsic part of the financial strategy of many independent colleges and is important for marketing strategy as well. The endowment is also valuable as a symbol representing faith in the continued existence of the institution.

Calculation Worksheet

	Fiscal year ending:	1976	1977	1978	1979	1980	1981	1982
A.	Endowment (including quasi) market value (35*)	$_____	$_____	$_____	$_____	$_____	$_____	$_____
B.	E&G + MT (23*)	$_____	$_____	$_____	$_____	$_____	$_____	$_____
C.	**Endowment Ratio (A divided by B):**	_____	_____	_____	_____	_____	_____	_____

*Refers to corresponding item on worksheet in chapter 3, "User Data."

Median Values for Similar Institutions

FTE ≤ 1500, from
Liberal Arts Colleges II

	1976	1977	1978	1979	1980	1981	1982
Endowment Ratio (17 institutions)	.551	.602	.594	.613			

Source: Audited financial statements coded to NACUBO standards, John Minter Associates, Boulder, Colorado.

Explanation of Calculations

Endowment funds can be invested in a broad range of items including cash, stocks, bonds, treasury bills, land, farms, oil wells, and commercial properties. Because of the variety of investment possibilities, it is difficult to find a measure that evaluates the potential effect of the endowment fund on the institution, though current market value closely approximates the economic value of the fund. By dividing the market value of the endowment by the amount of the unrestricted and restricted expenditures, the endowment can be compared with annual expenditures.

Interpretations

Endowment ratios compared to the national median for peer institutions. Institutions below the median may be at a competitive disadvantage, unless other resources or revenue flows (gifts or contributed services) provide comparable amounts of revenue. Low endowments generally mean the institution's priorities for current revenues and gifts have been concentrated on immediate support of budget operations. Until current operations are stabilized and intermediate reserves are accumulated, endowment-building should probably have low priority.

Declining ratios. Either or both of two problems may be in evidence. First, the institution's expenditures may be growing faster than the endowment. The ratio will thus decline, showing that the ability of the endowment to provide support to the budget is not keeping up with inflation. Second, the value of the endowment may be eroding because of unsuccessful investment policies, transfers out of quasi-endowment, or high payout rates.

Increasing ratios. Apparently the institution has had success in increasing the endowment through gifts or sound investment. The endowment has been growing at a faster rate than current fund expenditures.

Limitations

This ratio measures only superficially the overall health of the institution. Having an endowment does little to forestall financial difficulties, although some institutions have pledged endowment investments against loans.

There are many other factors to consider when assessing the long-range financial health of an institution. For example, the endowments of colleges affiliated with a religion may be supplemented by contributed services. A steady flow of expendable gifts from the religious order may have the same long-term financial effect as an endowment.

Because of fluctuating interest rates, the yield on endowment varies from year to year for many institutions.

Further Analysis

A declining ratio warrants a more thorough investigation. Payout rate, investment policies, and fund-raising programs should be reviewed. The following definitions will be useful in that analysis:

Rate of return: Return on investment as a percentage of market value at beginning of year, including appreciation and depreciation.
Payout rate: Earnings used as a percentage of market value at beginning of year.
Gifts rate: Gifts to endowment as a percentage of market value at beginning of year.
Growth rate of expenditures: Percentage increase in E&G + MT.

The analysis of these items involves the following calculation: Rate of return + gift rate − payout rate = growth in endowment market value. For the **Endowment Ratio** to remain steady, the growth of endowment market value must equal the growth of E&G + MT. This breakdown of endowment growth factors allows a year-by-year look at endowment policy and reveals damaging trends in gifts, payout, and return.

Some institutions may wish to set up a 15-year history of the ratio. The declining role of endowments in financial strategies can be vividly displayed by such a review.

Category: **Financial Resources**
Selected Statistic:
   Hidden Financial Resources
   (estimated only)

Significance of Statistic

Many institutions have financial resources that are not evident in the three previous sets of calculations. Institutions in urban areas may own valuable and perhaps unneeded land that should be considered a resource. Other institutions may be affiliated with financially sound organizations that would support them in a financial emergency, and others may have wealthy benefactors who provide continuing or growing support. To complement the analysis of financial resources, hidden resources should be compared with the size of the budget (E&G + MT). In general, the historical perspective is unnecessary, except where substantial changes have occurred (for example, the sale of a large piece of property). The hidden resources listed below (items B and D) are illustrative; administrators should add others that are appropriate.

Calculation Worksheet

	Fiscal year ending:	1976	1977	1978	1979	1980	1981	1982
A.	E&G + MT (23*)	$___	$___	$___	$___	$___	$___	$___
B.	Value of marketable land (not included in endowment) (36*)	$___	$___	$___	$___	$___	$___	$___
C.	Hidden Resources Ratio (B divided by A):	___	___	___	___	___	___	___
D.	Financial support from affiliated organizations or patron foundations (11*)	$___	$___	$___	$___	$___	$___	$___
E.	Hidden Resources Ratio (D divided by A):	___	___	___	___	___	___	___

*Refers to corresponding item on worksheet in chapter 3, "User Data."

Median Values for Similar Institutions: Not available.

Explanation of Calculations

After comparing these hidden resources with the institution's budget (E&G + MT), administrators may have a more complete understanding of the institution's total financial resources.

Limitations

Proceeds from the sale of large items such as land often can be added only to the endowment fund. The favorable effect on the institution may not be immediate since support comes solely from earnings. Because hidden resources have only long-term effect, ratios derived from those resources should be compared with the **Endowment Ratio**.

Further Analysis

Other hidden resources may be assessed by an actuarial valuation of known bequests and annuities, for example.

Flexibility: Indicators and Calculations

A. Debt Service to Revenue Ratio

Calculation: $$\frac{\text{Debt service due}}{\text{Current fund revenues}}$$

B. Acceptance Rate*

Calculation: $$\frac{\text{Acceptances of freshman and transfer applicants}}{\text{Freshman and transfer applications}}$$

or

$$\frac{\text{Acceptances of freshman and transfer applicants}}{\text{Inquiries}}$$

C. Tenured Faculty Ratio

Calculation: $$\frac{\text{Number of tenured faculty or faculty with long-term contracts (greater than five years)}}{\text{FTE faculty (fall)}}$$

*Core Statistic

Category: **Flexibility**
Selected Statistic:
   Debt Service to Revenue Ratio

Significance of Statistic

This ratio measures the flexibility of the institution to commit revenues to resources rather than to debt service. The higher the burden of debt service, the more difficulty the institution will have in finding sufficient revenue to allocate to other financial and nonfinancial needs. The failure to meet debt service is an admission of severe financial difficulty.

Calculation Worksheet

Fiscal year ending:		1976	1977	1978	1979	1980	1981	1982
A. Debt service due for all funds (within the fiscal year listed)	(27*)	$_____	$_____	$_____	$_____	$_____	$_____	$_____
B. Current fund revenues (restricted and unrestricted)	(9*)	$_____	$_____	$_____	$_____	$_____	$_____	$_____
C. **Debt Service to Revenue Ratio** (A divided by B):		_____	_____	_____	_____	_____	_____	_____

*Refers to corresponding item on worksheet in chapter 3, "User Data."

Median Values for Similar Institutions

FTE ≤ 1500, from Liberal Arts Colleges II

	1976	1977	1978	1979	1980	1981	1982
Debt Service to Revenue Ratio (28 institutions)	.012	.008	.005	.005			

Source: Audited financial statements coded to NACUBO standards, John Minter Associates, Boulder, Colorado.

Explanation of Calculations

Debt service for all funds is included to provide a complete picture of commitments to lenders. Debt service includes principal and interest payments as well as sinking fund obligations. Even if a moratorium has allowed the suspension of debt repayment, the amount normally due for the year should be shown in order to establish a true trend.

Restricted current fund revenues are added to unrestricted current fund revenues so that a comparison of *total* revenue inflow to debt service commitments is possible.

Interpretations

Increasing ratios. Budgeting flexibility decreases as debt service commitments increase. More institutional resources must go toward debt repayment.

Decreasing ratios. Flexibility increases as debt service commitments decline. The institution may commit these funds to other purposes.

Limitations

No national standards for budget percentage dedicated to debt service may be inferred from the median values. The willingness and ability to commit revenues to debt service vary greatly among institutions.

Further Analysis

Any trend in debt service burden is revealed by analyzing the following:
- Unsecured debt repayment
- Secured debt repayment

If growth is occurring in the unsecured component, the institution may be greatly increasing the risk of future financial difficulty.

Core Statistic

Category: **Flexibility**
Selected Statistic:
   Acceptance Rate

Significance of Statistic

This is the ratio of first-time student acceptances (freshmen and transfers) to the total number of applications. As this ratio increases and the institution accepts a greater percentage of applicants, the probability is greater that the college will be affected by fluctuations in student markets. Institutions that accept a high percentage of their applicants have less flexibility to increase enrollments should the number of applicants fall. (Projected U.S. population trends indicate declining numbers of 18- to 21-year-olds.)

Though accepting students who are less prepared creates obvious problems for institutions, it is important to emphasize that the **Acceptance Rate** is used as a measure of flexibility, not of institutional quality.

Calculation Worksheet

	Academic year ending:	1976	1977	1978	1979	1980	1981	1982
A.	Acceptances of freshmen and transfer applicants (44*)	_____	_____	_____	_____	_____	_____	_____
B.	Freshmen and transfer applications (or) (42*/43*)							
	Inquiries (see **Explanation,** p. 25) (41*)	_____	_____	_____	_____	_____	_____	_____
C.	**Acceptance Rate (A divided by B):**	_____	_____	_____	_____	_____	_____	_____

*Refers to corresponding item on worksheet in chapter 3, "User Data."

Median Values for Similar Institutions: Not available.

Explanation of Calculations

Acceptances should include freshmen and transfers. *Applications* in the denominator should be for the same freshmen or transfer places counted in the numerator. In other words, *applications* should be from the *previous* year.

If there is substantial preapplication counseling, *inquiries* should be used in the denominator since the institution is probably guaranteeing admission after the counseling. In those cases, the number of *inquiries* is the closest approximation of available and interested students. Purchased "lists" of students should not be included in *inquiries*.

Interpretations

High ratios. **Acceptance Rates** approaching 100 percent indicate little flexibility in the college's admissions practices. In such cases there is little possibility of maintaining enrollments by "lowering standards." Other forms of contingency protection such as larger financial reserves may be needed.

Limitations

A crucial factor missing from the interpretation of the **Acceptance Rate** is the probability that the actual number of applications will decline. Only part of the ability of the institution to respond to a decline is measured above. Gauging the adequacy of financial reserves hinges for most institutions on an estimate of (1) the maximum decline in enrollments, (2) the net effect on revenue of the projected decline, and (3) the number of years of lag-time needed to adjust expenses to the reduced enrollment level. Reserves can be used for a short period to ease the financial problems caused by decreasing enrollments.

The trend of students applying to more schools may show up as a false decrease in risk. The potential yield to each institution declines as students choose to send out more applications. Few data showing changes in student application behavior are available, although groups of institutions can and do share **Acceptance** and **Yield Rates** to assist each other in measuring student application changes.

Further Analysis

The following definitions are also helpful in amplifying any trends that are discovered:

Rejection rates. The proportion of applicants actually rejected by the college. This may not complement the **Acceptance Rate** if incomplete applications have been counted as applications.

Yield rates. The proportion of accepted students who choose to attend.

Market share. The ratio of the college's first-time enrollments to the first-time enrollments of the top 10 competitors.

Projected applications. High school graduations projected by geographic region.

Category: **Flexibility**
Selected Statistic:
Tenured Faculty Ratio

Significance of Statistic

The relative inflexibility of the budget intensifies the need for financial resources, especially endowment. Budget inflexibility may occur when expenditures such as long-term salary contracts take an increased share of the budget. These expenditures limit the institutional manager's ability to change long-term budget composition. The statistic that most easily monitors institutional flexibility with regard to faculty is the **Tenured Faculty Ratio**. Normally, an institution must declare and prove financial exigency to release tenured faculty. Institutions with increasing proportions of tenured faculty may be able to offset this increased inflexibility with high levels of relatively stable revenues such as endowment income or annual fund giving.

Calculation Worksheet

	Fiscal year ending:	1976	1977	1978	1979	1980	1981	1982
A.	Number of tenured faculty or faculty with long-term contracts (greater than five years) (38*)							
B.	FTE faculty (fall) (39*)							
C.	Tenured Faculty Ratio (A divided by B):							

*Refers to corresponding item on worksheet in chapter 3, "User Data."

Median Values for Similar Institutions

FTE ≤ 1500, from Liberal Arts Colleges II

	1976	1977	1978	1979	1980	1981	1982
Tenured Faculty Ratio (20 institutions)	.430	.432	.450	.375			

Source: Audited financial statements coded to NACUBO standards, John Minter Associates, Boulder, Colorado.

Explanation of Calculations

While most tenured faculty are full-time, total faculty full-time equivalents will include part-time faculty. The use of FTE faculty in the denominator is necessary because the ratio monitors changes in the proportion of *all* faculty holding tenure.

Interpretations

Tenured Faculty Ratios indicate changes in the flexibility to make budget reductions.

Limitations

Many other commitments serve to decrease budget flexibility, including debt service, insurance, salaries of key administrators, employee benefits, and utilities expenditures.

Further Analysis

If the analyst is greatly concerned about trends in budget flexibility, a more detailed analysis is possible. First, the budget should be divided according to degree of commitment into major expenditure categories. Then the analyst should rank the categories according to the degree of flexibility for the next five years. The ranking might begin with tenured faculty salaries and benefits, debt service, utilities, other faculty salaries, top administrative salaries, commitments for services (insurance, etc.), other salaries, and other expenditures. This breakdown might be displayed on bar graphs showing changes in the budget proportion dedicated to the various expenditure categories.

Category: **Flexibility**
Selected Statistic:
  Hidden Financial Risks

Significance of Statistic

Generally, the occurrence of these hidden financial risks varies greatly among institutions. Risks covered on the following worksheet include projected enrollment declines, increases in uncollectible student accounts, and student receivables.

The larger such contingencies loom on the institution's horizon, the more necessary it becomes to build financial reserves. External forces such as enrollment declines or funding interruptions can have an important effect on financial strategies.

Calculation Worksheet

	Fiscal year ending:	1981	1982	1983	1984	1985
Effect of Potential Enrollment Decline						
A.	Potential *first-time* student enrollment decline (% decline from base year 1980 because of changing demographics) (57*)	____%	____%	____%	____%	____%
B.	Effect on *overall* enrollment (% decline from base year 1980 because of changing demographics)	____%	____%	____%	____%	____%
C.	**Effect in terms of current tuition dollars (or total dollars lost) (multiply B by item 1*):**	$____	$____	$____	$____	$____

*Refers to corresponding item on worksheet in chapter 3, "User Data."

Median Values for Similar Institutions: Not Available

	Fiscal year ending:	1976	1977	1978	1979	1980	1981	1982
Effect of Uncollectibles								
D.	Uncollectible student accounts written off in fiscal year. (31*)	$____	$____	$____	$____	$____	$____	$____
E.	E&G + MT (23*)	$____	$____	$____	$____	$____	$____	$____
F.	**Uncollectibles to E&G + MT (D divided by E):**	____	____	____	____	____	____	____

*Refers to corresponding item on worksheet in chapter 3, "User Data."

Median Values for Similar Institutions: Not Available

Fiscal year ending:		1976	1977	1978	1979	1980	1981	1982
Student Receivables Ratio								
G. Student accounts receivable at end of fiscal year (not including credit balances or advance billings)	(30*)	$_____	$_____	$_____	$_____	$_____	$_____	$_____
H. Tuition and fees	(1*)	$_____	$_____	$_____	$_____	$_____	$_____	$_____
I. Auxiliary enterprise revenue	(7*)	$_____	$_____	$_____	$_____	$_____	$_____	$_____
J. Total student billings (approx.) (add H and I)		$_____	$_____	$_____	$_____	$_____	$_____	$_____
K. **Student Receivables to Billings Ratio** (G divided by J):		_____	_____	_____	_____	_____	_____	_____

*Refers to corresponding item on worksheet in chapter 3, "User Data."

Median Values for Similar Institutions   Private four-year colleges

	1976	1977	1978	1979	1980	1981	1982
Student Receivables to Billings Ratio	.034			.039			

Source: Higher Education Panel Report 49, American Council on Education, 1981.

Explanation of Calculations

State-by-state demographic data showing declines in the 18- to 25-year-old population through 1990 are available from the Policy Analysis Service of the American Council on Education. Some institutions know the high school graduation potential of their primary recruitment locations. Recent high school graduates, traditionally part of the 18- to 25-year-old group, no longer comprise the entire first-time enrollment group. Because the size of other age groups will remain relatively steady through 1990, the decreasing size of the 18- to 25-year-old group does not necessarily mean that actual first-time enrollments will decline. (Only "potential decline" is under consideration.) First-time enrollments are only a part of overall enrollments, and a set of projected institutional attrition ratios should allow calculation of the overall potential enrollment declines. The computed enrollment decline percentage, when applied to current tuition revenues, will show in current dollars the potential overall dollar effect of the decline. Enrollment declines that result from competitive programs now available at peer institutions should not be ignored in these estimates.

Rules vary from institution to institution as to when a student account becomes uncollectible. In determining this statistic, the advice of the institution's auditors should be followed.

"Student accounts receivable" should not include credit balances or advance billings. This will allow an accurate assessment of the amount unpaid from previous billings.

Interpretations

The larger the potential decline in enrollments, the more the institution should be preparing to build financial resources, reassess marketing strategies, and plan budget reduction possibilities.

The probability rises that total revenues for the year are overstated as the proportion of student revenues outstanding at year-end grows. Increases in this proportion indicate either a problem in collection procedures or a change in the ability and willingness of students to pay. This may signal a trend in decreased student financial responsibility as well as an increase in the risk of cash-flow problems. Since students who drop out may be less willing to finish payment of their accounts, decreases in retention may accompany the increases in unpaid accounts.

Growing unpaid accounts may also stem from schedule changes, difficulties with federal and state aid programs, and shifts from semester to quarter systems or vice versa.

Limitations

Enrollment projections are not based on actual data. The true outcomes remain unknown, and there is much debate about the size of future enrollments.

Also, a change of auditors may cause a change in the rules for write-offs and may make year-to-year comparisons uncertain.

Further Analysis

Measurable risks not covered on the worksheet include pending litigation, potential interruptions of funds from state or federal sources or from gifts, and large unplanned expenditure increases for items such as utilities.

Nonfinancial Resources: Indicators and Calculations

A. Student Characteristics
1. Average test scores of entering freshmen
2. Selectivity (same as **Acceptance Rate**)
3. Percentage of entering students from top 20% of high school class
4. Percentage of entering students from top 40% of high school class

B. Institutional Attraction
1. Yield Rate

    Calculation: $$\frac{\text{New students (freshmen and transfers)}}{\text{Acceptances of freshmen and transfer applicants}}$$

2. Retention:

    Calculation: Percentage of previous year's eligible students who enroll for next class

3. Student Services Expenditures per Student

    Calculation: $$\frac{\text{Student services expenditures**}}{\text{Total student headcount (fall)}}$$

C. Academic Program
1. Instruction Proportion*

    Calculation: $$\frac{\text{Instruction expenditures}}{\text{E\&G + MT minus restricted fund scholarships}}$$

2. Instruction per FTE Student*

    Calculation: $$\frac{\text{Instruction expenditures**}}{\text{FTE students (fall)}}$$

D. Faculty
1. Change in Average Compensation*

    Calculation: Average full-time faculty compensation***

2. Student to Faculty Ratio*

    Calculation: $$\frac{\text{FTE students}}{\text{FTE faculty}}$$

E. Staff

   Calculation: $$\frac{\text{Total student headcount (fall)}}{\text{FTE administrative exempt staff (excluding auxiliary staff)}}$$

F. Deferred Physical Plant Maintenance

   Calculation: $$\frac{\text{Estimate of deferred physical plant maintenance}}{\text{E\&G + MT}}$$

*Core Statistic
**Deflated by Higher Education Price Index (HEPI): 1971=1.00
***Deflated by Consumer Price Index (CPI): 1971=1.00

Category: **Nonfinancial Resources**
Selected Statistic:
   Student Characteristics

Significance of Statistic

Changes in student characteristics can materially affect the nature and mission of the institution.

No value judgment is made about the proper direction of change for the student characteristics measured (test scores and selectivity, for example). Declines in the following indicators may reflect a relative decrease in the ability or effort to attract students whose preparation matches that of previous students. Such declines may also result from increased competition or decreased availability of students.

Calculation Worksheet

Academic year ending:		1976	1977	1978	1979	1980	1981	1982
A. Selectivity (same as **Acceptance Rate**, p. 24)		_____	_____	_____	_____	_____	_____	_____
B. Average test scores of entering freshmen	(47*)	_____	_____	_____	_____	_____	_____	_____
C. Percentage of entering students from top 20% of high school class	(48*)	_____%	_____%	_____%	_____%	_____%	_____%	_____%
D. Percentage of entering students from top 40% of high school class	(49*)	_____%	_____%	_____%	_____%	_____%	_____%	_____%

*Refers to corresponding item on worksheet in chapter 3, "User Data."

Median Values for Similar Institutions

FTE ≤ 1500, from Liberal Arts Colleges II

Academic year ending:	1976	1977	1978	1979	1980	1981	1982
Percentage of entering students from top 20% of high school class (15 institutions)		32%	33%	34%	35%		
Percentage of entering students from top 40% of high school class (15 institutions)		48%	57%	59%	63%		

Source: Audited financial statements coded to NACUBO standards, John Minter Associates, Boulder, Colorado.

Explanation of Calculations

Either SAT or ACT scores or a composite may be used. (See the following tables.) Year-to-year consistency is most important.

See pages 24-25 for an explanation of the selectivity (**Acceptance Rate**) calculation.

SAT Score Averages for College-Bound Seniors, 1975-1979

	Verbal			Mathematical		
	Male	Female	Total	Male	Female	Total
1975	437	431	434	495	449	472
1976	433	430	431	497	446	472
1977	431	427	429	497	445	470
1978	433	425	429	494	444	468
1979	431	423	427	493	443	467

Source: "National College-Bound Seniors," 1979 Admissions Testing Program of the College Board, Princeton, New Jersey, 1979.

ACT Means and SDs* for Successive Years of Tested College-Bound Students

	Total (males and females combined)											
	English		Math		Social Studies		Natural Science		Composition				
Year	Mean	SD	Mean	SD	Mean	SD	Mean	SD	Mean	SD	Males	Females	Total
1975-76	17.2	5.5	17.1	7.7	16.6	7.4	20.4	6.6	17.9	5.9	412,717	475,358	888,075
1976-77	17.3	5.4	16.8	7.9	16.9	7.4	20.4	6.6	18.0	6.0	388,891	458,711	847,602
1977-78	17.4	5.5	16.8	7.8	16.6	7.3	20.4	6.6	17.9	6.0	401,670	481,360	883,030
1978-79	17.5	5.5	16.9	7.6	16.7	7.3	20.6	6.4	18.1	5.8	408,666	487,579	896,245

*Standard deviation

Source: "Class Profile Service," The American College Testing Program, Iowa City, Iowa, 1980.

Interpretations

Declines in selectivity and achievement. One interpretation of declines in freshmen entering average test scores and selectivity is that insufficient funds have been allocated to recruitment and to various "attracting" resources such as athletics, the academic program, and the campus environment.

These resources should be separately analyzed to determine if they are causing declines in the preparation of students, as measured by selectivity and test scores.

Changes in competing peer institutions, demographic shifts, and swings in social values all have the potential to diminish the relative worth of attracting resources. These external changes should be monitored to complete the interpretation of shifts in student characteristics.

Limitations

Any "quality" measure such as test scores or selectivity can be misleading. Test scores measure test performance very effectively and student suitability for college less effectively. Also, national trends in test scores should be considered.

Many institutions are justifiably more interested in what they can do for students than in the caliber of students recruited. These institutions do not depend on test scores as an indicator of student suitability. Trends in test scores merely reflect changes in precollege preparation of the pool of students usually drawn to the college.

Further Analysis

Changes in the total enrollment and in the composition of students (including age and interests) are also important. For example, older students may have lower test scores but may be a major addition to the institution.

Category: **Nonfinancial Resources**
Selected Statistic:
Institutional Attraction

Significance of Statistic

Another important resource is represented by institutional attraction and indirectly by **Student Services Expenditures per Student**. The ability of the institution to draw and hold students is a function of academic programs, reputation, available student services, competition, recruiting, and the types of students it has historically drawn. Deterioration in the following proxies signals a decline in the core activities of the institution as perceived by current and potential students.

Calculation Worksheet

Academic year ending:		1976	1977	1978	1979	1980	1981	1982
Yield Rate								
A. New students (freshmen and transfers)	(45*)	___	___	___	___	___	___	___
B. Acceptances of freshman and transfer applicants	(44*)	___	___	___	___	___	___	___
C. Yield Rate (A divided by B):		___%	___%	___%	___%	___%	___%	___%
Retention								
D. Percentage of previous year's eligible students who enroll for next class:	(46*)	___%	___%	___%	___%	___%	___%	___%
Student Services								
E. Total student headcount (fall)	(51*)	___	___	___	___	___	___	___
F. Student services expenditures	(17*)	$___	$___	$___	$___	$___	$___	$___
G. Higher Education Price Index (1971 = 1.00)		1.379	1.468	1.567	1.689	1.856	___	___
H. Deflated student services expenditures (F divided by G):		$___	$___	$___	$___	$___	$___	$___
I. Constant (1971) Dollar Student Services Expenditures per Student (H divided by E):		$___	$___	$___	$___	$___	$___	$___

*Refers to corresponding item on worksheet in chapter 3, "User Data."

Median Values for Similiar Institutions

FTE ≤ 1500, from Liberal Arts Colleges II

Academic year ending:	1976	1977	1978	1979	1980	1981	1982
Yield Rate (freshmen and transfers) (18 institutions)		1.2	1.4	1.4	1.3		
Constant (1971) Dollar Student Services Expenditures per Student (27 institutions)	$243.50	$253.20	$255.60	$242.30			

Source: Audited financial statements coded to NACUBO standards, John Minter Associates, Boulder, Colorado.

Explanation of Calculations

The NACUBO definition for student services functions is given in appendix B.

Acceptances should be comparable to the group of applicants so the **Yield Rate** is calculated with consistent data. There are many ways to calculate retention (for example, with or without dropouts or returning students). Because of the lack of annual national data, any convenient and consistent method is appropriate for internal comparisons.

Dividing by the Higher Education Price Index (HEPI) removes the effect of inflation on expenditures. Dividing by the headcount provides an estimate of the level of service available to each student.

Interpretations

Declines. A decline in retention may indicate an erosion in the attractiveness of the institution. Such erosion could be caused by a decline in student services or in other resources that build student commitments. Also, the institution may be attracting students less likely to be retained.

Increases. Students are being attracted to and are staying with the institution.

Limitations

In many cases changes in retention rates are affected more by the type of student recruited and by student options such as work and competing schools than by institutional decisions or actions.

The student service function contains many expenditures of limited benefit to students and is not solely responsible for changes in retention. For example, the effect of greater federal reporting requirements for student aid will show up as an increase in expenditures, whereas the effect of this particular expenditure on short-run student retention is probably negligible.

Retention figures may be misleading if academic dismissals are mixed with dropout statistics. Declining retention, if caused by increased academic dismissals, may in fact signal potentially improved conditions for drawing and holding students.

Further Analysis

Retention problems call for a set of detailed analyses beyond the scope of this workbook. Examples are exit interviews, follow-up studies of students who leave, and attitude surveys.

Decreases in **Student Services Expenditures per Student** may be analyzed further by following trends in the separate budgets (per student) of financial aid, counseling, infirmary, and other offices in student services. It may also be helpful to include dormitory counselors in the analysis if their cost is normally charged to auxiliary services.

Core Statistics
(E and I below)

Category: Nonfinancial Resources
Selected Statistic:
Academic Program—
Instruction Proportion,
Instruction per FTE Student

Significance of Statistic

Institutions struggling with enrollment and fund-raising problems may be neglecting the academic program, their most important resource. The purpose of this statistic is to determine if the college has been maintaining the allocation of resources to the academic program.

The proportion of the budget spent on instruction indicates the institution's sense of priority for this activity. In many cases priority is affected by the need to intensify the fund-raising program and emphasize recruiting activity. Comparisons with peer institutions and a history of the instruction budget's role will show the extent to which the college is capable of protecting and enhancing its academic resources.

Calculation Worksheet

		Fiscal year ending:	1976	1977	1978	1979	1980	1981	1982
A.	Instruction	(13*)	$____	$____	$____	$____	$____	$____	$____
B.	E&G + MT	(23*)	$____	$____	$____	$____	$____	$____	$____
C.	Scholarships and fellowships from restricted funds	(21*)	$____	$____	$____	$____	$____	$____	$____
D.	E&G + MT minus scholarships and fellowships from restricted funds (B minus C)		$____	$____	$____	$____	$____	$____	$____
E.	**Instruction Proportion (A divided by D):**		____%	____%	____%	____%	____%	____%	____%
F.	Higher Education Price Index (1971 = 1.00)		1.379	1.468	1.567	1.689	1.856	____	____
G.	Instruction in constant (1971) dollars (A divided by F)		$____	$____	$____	$____	$____	$____	$____
H.	FTE students (fall)	(50*)	____	____	____	____	____	____	____
I.	**Instruction per FTE Student in Constant (1971) Dollars (G divided by H):**		$____	$____	$____	$____	$____	$____	$____

*Refers to corresponding item on worksheet in chapter 3, "User Data."

Median Values for Similar Institutions

FTE ≤ 1500, from Liberal Arts Colleges II

	1976	1977	1978	1979	1980	1981	1982
Instruction Proportion** (28 institutions)	42.3%	42.1%	41.7%	40.4%			
Instruction per FTE Student in Constant (1971) Dollars (27 institutions)	$955.30	$944.60	$870.70	$921.00			

**Less restricted and unrestricted scholarships and fellowships.
Source: Audited financial statements coded to NACUBO standards, John Minter Associates, Boulder, Colorado.

Explanation of Calculations

Restricted scholarships, whether federal or institutional, are not included in the calculation because they are not measures of institutional activity and, if included, would distort the calculation. For example, because some institutions record BEOGs in current funds rather than in agency funds, removing BEOGs from the calculation enhances consistency.

Interpretations

Decreasing proportion. Less emphasis on instruction means the institution has been distributing its revenues away from its primary function. If previous statistics have shown increasing financial reserves, then a declining **Instruction Proportion** may show that the apparent prosperity has not come from increased revenues but perhaps from a diversion of funds.

In institutions with declining financial resources, decreases in the **Instruction Proportion** may also occur because of greater demands for administrative expenditures such as admissions or fund raising.

Decreasing instructional costs per student. When instructional costs per student decline, students are receiving less (on a cost basis) from the academic program. In many cases this may be an indication of improved operation and is quite acceptable. In other cases it may indicate academic program cutbacks.

Increases. More resources are being accumulated in the academic program compared to the overall budget. Another possibility is that the number of students has not increased. If the institution remains financially strong elsewhere, this is a positive indication of increased commitment of resources to the primary program.

Limitations

A decrease in instruction expenditures as a proportion of the operating budget may not indicate an absolute decline. **Instruction Proportion** and **Instruction per FTE Student** must be viewed together. The most severe limitation of these statistics is their inability to measure changes in quality. Increasing operating efficiency may result in overall quality increases even though the statistics show decline.

Further Analysis

Analysis of the absolute change in academic offerings and in the efficiency of the academic program is also possible. The following questions briefly outline this analysis:

- How many degree credit majors have been offered each year? (Changes in this number indicate absolute program changes.)
- How many courses are listed per enrolling student? Course proliferation indicates decreasing efficiency but is somewhat beneficial to the overall program. Course proliferation is a problem, however, when the level of academic resources is constant.
- What proportion of course sections have 50 or more students? What proportion have six or fewer? (Changes in these two proportions may indicate changes in the efficiency of course offerings as measured by the proportion of very small or very large classes.)

Core Statistic

Category: **Nonfinancial Resources**
Selected Statistic:
Faculty—Change in Average Compensation, Student to Faculty Ratio

Significance of Statistic

Faculty is another institutional resource.

By measuring average faculty salary trends and the **Student to Faculty Ratio**, the analyst is able to compare faculty trends to trends in other resources.

Many decisions faced by administrators are resource allocation decisions. The faculty statistics may indicate that more resources should be allocated to areas such as faculty compensation or the number of faculty.

Calculation Worksheet

	Fiscal year ending:	1976	1977	1978	1979	1980	1981	1982
A.	Average full-time faculty compensation (salary and benefits) (25*)	$___	$___	$___	$___	$___	$___	$___
B.	Consumer Price Index (1971 = 1.00)	1.396	1.477	1.577	1.750	___	___	___
C.	Full-time faculty compensation in constant (1971) dollars (A divided by B)	$___	$___	$___	$___	$___	$___	$___
D.	**Change from previous year:**		___%	___%	___%	___%	___%	___%
E.	FTE students (fall) (50*)	___	___	___	___	___	___	___
F.	FTE faculty (fall) (39*)	___	___	___	___	___	___	___
G.	**Student to Faculty Ratio (E divided by F):**	___	___	___	___	___	___	___

* Refers to corresponding item on worksheet in chapter 3, "User Data."

Median Values for Similar Institutions

FTE ≤ 1500, from Liberal Arts Colleges II

	1976	1977	1978	1979	1980	1981	1982
Average full-time faculty compensation** (14 institutions)	$13,616	$15,155	$16,316	$17,190			
Full-time faculty compensation in constant (1971) dollars (14 institutions)	$9,873	$10,317	$10,412	$10,178			
Change from previous year (14 institutions)		+4.5%	+.009%	−2.2%			
Student to Faculty Ratio (20 institutions)	14.9	15.6	15.6	16.3			

**Compensation = salary + fringe benefits.
Source: Audited financial statements coded to NACUBO standards, John Minter Associates, Boulder, Colorado.

Faculty Pay*: Year-to-Year Increases in Average Salaries and the Effect of Inflation

Academic years:	'75-'76	'76-'77	'77-'78	'78-'79	'79-'80
In current dollars:					
Professor	+6.2%	+4.7%	+5.2%	+5.6%	+7.5%
Associate	+5.9%	+4.7%	+5.4%	+5.8%	+7.0%
Assistant	+5.7%	+4.7%	+5.3%	+5.9%	+6.8%
Instructor	+6.1%	+4.7%	+5.4%	+6.0%	+6.4%
All ranks	+6.0%	+4.7%	+5.3%	+6.0%	+7.1%
After adjusting for inflation:					
Professor	−0.8%	−1.0%	−1.4%	−3.5%	−5.3%
Associate	−1.1%	−1.0%	−1.2%	−3.3%	−5.7%
Assistant	−1.3%	−1.0%	−1.3%	−3.2%	−5.9%
Instructor	−0.9%	−1.0%	−1.2%	−3.1%	−6.3%
All ranks	−1.0%	−1.0%	−1.3%	−3.1%	−5.6%

*For institutions reporting comparable data for each one-year period since 1969-70.

Source: "Annual Report on the Economic Status of the Profession, 1979-80," *Academe: Bulletin of the American Association of University Professors,* Washington, D.C., AAUP, September 1980.

Explanation of Calculations

The Consumer Price Index was used to demonstrate changes in faculty purchasing power.

Interpretations

No increase in constant dollar compensation. Zero percent increase means average faculty compensation matched inflation.

Negative compensation increases. Compensation has not kept up with inflation. The resource may be eroding.

Positive compensation growth. The resource is being maintained and improved. (Even if faculty salaries at all institutions increase more than inflation, however, other sectors of the economy may be luring some of the best faculty.)

Changes in Student to Faculty Ratio. Changes here should be in step with changes in instructional expenditures per FTE student.

Limitations

Faculty compensation changes may not always reflect changes in efficiency of instructional delivery or changes in quality. Effective instruction can be measured only by much more complex tools. The **Student to Faculty Ratio** suffers from the same limitations. The ratio can show only problems created by inflation's effect on real salaries or by the inordinate growth of average class sizes.

Turnover savings are masked by measuring average faculty compensation for both continuing and new faculty. Continuing faculty may be receiving adequate increases. Nonetheless, if average faculty salaries are down, the salary of the institution's "typical" faculty member may be slipping in purchasing power and in prestige, when compared with the pay of other workers in the economy. An erosion of overall faculty quality could result as faculty members are drawn away to other sectors of the economy.

Further Analysis

Analysis of the salary growth of continuing faculty can be facilitated by assembling AAUP/HEGIS faculty salary questionnaires from several years. Annual compensation changes can be calculated for each rank of continuing faculty.

Trends in **Student to Faculty Ratios** may be further analyzed by calculating (for each academic discipline) student credit hours generated per FTE faculty member. This allows isolation of particular departments most responsible for various trends.

The proportion of part-time faculty among total full-time equivalents can also be important. Shifts toward more part-time faculty may suggest major changes in campus atmosphere and increases in budget flexibility.

Category: **Nonfinancial Resources**
Selected Statistic:
    Staff—Students to FTE
    Administrative Exempt Staff Ratio

Significance of Statistic.

Those responsible for administering the institution are another measurable resource. Increases in the number of staff may explain some other trends, especially declines in instruction as a proportion of total expenditures.

Calculation Worksheet

	Fiscal year ending:	1976	1977	1978	1979	1980	1981	1982
A.	Total student headcount (fall) (51*)	_____	_____	_____	_____	_____	_____	_____
B.	FTE administrative exempt staff (excluding auxiliary staff) (fall) (40*)	_____	_____	_____	_____	_____	_____	_____
C.	**Students to FTE Administrative Exempt Staff Ratio (A divided by B):**	_____	_____	_____	_____	_____	_____	_____

* Refers to corresponding item on worksheet in Chapter 3, "User Data."

Median Values for Similar Institutions: Not available.

Explanation of Calculations

Students to FTE Administrative Exempt Staff Ratios should be measured by using a consistent date such as October 15. Full-time equivalence for staff should be based on the portion of the work week committed to the institution. Residence and dining hall staff are not included. Hourly staff, called "nonexempt," are excluded to simplify this measure.

Headcount students are compared to administrative staff because of the administrative burden of each student, whether full- or part-time.

Student workers are not included unless their contribution is equivalent to regular staff contribution and their pay nearly equivalent to regular staff pay.

Interpretations

Changes in Students to FTE Administrative Exempt Staff Ratio. This ratio indicates changes in the burden of administering the college. If the ratio is increasing, efficiency may be increasing.

Limitations

No change in administrative quality or institutional effectiveness is actually measured. There are no known guides for measuring the adequacy of administration.

Further Analysis

Increases in administrative burden may explain many of the changes in staffing levels. It will be helpful to collect numbers for and observe trends in the following:

- Student applications
- Students applying for financial aid
- Financial transactions
- Payroll checks written
- Athletic events

Category: **Nonfinancial Resources**
Selected Statistic:
   Deferred Physical Plant Maintenance

Significance of Statistic

The condition of the physical plant should be monitored for a more comprehensive view of the condition of the institution's resources. Neglect of maintenance may have serious implications for health and safety and may create an unsightly campus that erodes an institution's ability to attract students.

Calculation Worksheet

	Fiscal year ending:	1976	1977	1978	1979	1980	1981	1982
A.	Estimate of deferred physical plant maintenance (37*)	$_____	$_____	$_____	$_____	$_____	$_____	$_____
B.	E&G + MT (23*)	$_____	$_____	$_____	$_____	$_____	$_____	$_____
C.	**Deferred Maintenance Ratio** (A divided by B):	_____	_____	_____	_____	_____	_____	_____

*Refers to corresponding item on worksheet in Chapter 3, "User Data."

Median Values for Similar Institutions: Not available.

Explanation of Calculations

To interpret this statistic properly, guidelines for the definition of deferred maintenance are necessary. The statistic should include all repairs undone at the end of the fiscal year. These are repairs that would normally have been done to keep buildings functional and that will have to be done eventually. Painting and roof or steam line repairs are obvious examples. Renovations should be included, especially if they are necessary for the continuation of an essential program. Accommodations for the handicapped should not be included unless the institution has made an irreversible commitment to make the campus accessible to handicapped students.

Another method of calculating deferred maintenance is to "zero-base budget" all renovation and repairs each year. Whatever is not funded in the budget is thus deferred.

Interpretations

Growth in Deferred Maintenance Ratio. By comparing the amount of deferred maintenance with the expenditure budget, a better understanding of the size of the former can be obtained. When the ratio represents a significant portion of the budget, it is clear that normal revenues will be unable to reduce building neglect.

Negligible Deferred Maintenance Ratio. Buildings are being maintained and preserved.

Limitations

No acceptable national standards for assessing deferred maintenance have been established. Clearly, some deferrals are more costly or more unsightly and dangerous than others. Some may also be in violation of building codes.

In an overall analysis of the operating budget, the importance of the ratio is reduced if institutions regard deferred maintenance problems as "outside the regular budget" and as the object of fund-raising campaigns.

Further Analysis

The following statistics may be useful in evaluating the physical plant as a resource:

- FTE students per net assignable square foot of building area. (Trends in this measure will show how the institution physically adapts to changes in the number of students.)

- Plant operations and maintenance costs (not including utilities) in constant dollars per gross area of buildings (in square feet). (This measure shows trends in "normal" maintenance budgets. At times, budget squeezes put extraordinary pressure on this function, resulting in a lengthening list of deferred maintenance projects.)

Category: **Nonfinancial Resources**
Selected Statistic:
    Hidden Nonfinancial Resources

Significance of Statistic

    This page is reserved for an estimate of hidden nonfinancial resources such as location, trustees, image, new programs, proximity to resources such as museums or cultural centers, and trends in perceptions of the institution's quality. Some hidden resources (excess capacity and changing regional economic conditions, for example) may have a negative effect.

Changes Affecting Financial Resources: Indicators and Calculations

A. Student-Derived Revenue Trends

1. Constant (1971) Dollar Net Student Revenue*

    Calculation: Tuition and fees minus scholarships and fellowships from unrestricted funds**

2. Constant (1971) Dollar Tuition Rate*/**

3. Financial FTE Enrollments*

    Calculation: $$\frac{\text{Net student revenue}}{\text{Tuition and fee rate per year for a full-time student}}$$

4. Tuition Discount Factor*

    Calculation: $$\frac{\text{Financial FTE enrollments}}{\text{FTE students}}$$

B. Government-Derived Inflow Proportion

Calculation: $$\frac{\text{Total government-related inflows}}{\text{Current fund revenues}}$$

C. Revenue Bar Graphs

- Tuition and fees
- Appropriations
- Grants and contracts
- Gifts
- Endowment income
- Other revenues

D. Contributed Services Ratio

Calculation: $$\frac{\text{Value of contributed services}}{\text{E\&G + MT}}$$

E. Expenditures per Student

Calculation: $$\frac{\text{E\&G+MT minus scholarships and fellowships from restricted funds**}}{\text{FTE students (fall)}}$$

F. Expenditures—Unit Trends

- Average exempt staff salaries
- Books and periodicals
- Utilities

G. Expenditure Bar Graphs

- Instruction
- Research
- Public service
- Academic support
- Student services
- Institutional support
- Operation and maintenance of plant
- Scholarships and fellowships (unrestricted only)
- Mandatory transfers

*Core Statistic
**Deflated by Higher Education Price Index (HEPI): 1971=1.00

Core Statistics
(F,H,J,M below)

Category: **Changes Affecting Financial Resources**
Selected Statistic:
Student-Derived Revenue Trends

Significance of Statistic

The stability of student-derived revenue depends on several factors: enrollment must remain level; the tuition rate must keep up with inflation; and student aid from unrestricted funds should not increase faster than inflation unless extra enrollments bring in sufficient revenue to cover the extra costs. A lack of strength in the indicator means the institution is no longer drawing revenue from students as it once did. It may be necessary to examine policies for tuition, recruitment, and student aid.

Calculation Worksheet

	Fiscal year ending:		1976	1977	1978	1979	1980	1981	1982
A.	Tuition and fees	(1*)	$_____	$_____	$_____	$_____	$_____	$_____	$_____
B.	Scholarships and fellowships from unrestricted funds	(20*)	$_____	$_____	$_____	$_____	$_____	$_____	$_____
C.	Net student revenue (A minus B)		$_____	$_____	$_____	$_____	$_____	$_____	$_____
D.	Tuition and fee rate per year for a full-time student	(12*)	$_____	$_____	$_____	$_____	$_____	$_____	$_____
E.	Higher Education Price Index (1971 = 1.00)		1.379	1.468	1.567	1.689	1.856	_____	_____
F.	Constant (1971) Dollar Net Student Revenue (C divided by E)		$_____	$_____	$_____	$_____	$_____	$_____	$_____
G.	**Change from previous year:**			_____%	_____%	_____%	_____%	_____%	_____%
H.	**Constant (1971) Dollar Tuition Rate** (D divided by E)		$_____	$_____	$_____	$_____	$_____	$_____	$_____
I.	**Constant (1971) dollar tuition change from previous year:**			_____%	_____%	_____%	_____%	_____%	_____%
J.	**Financial FTE Enrollments** (C divided by D):		_____	_____	_____	_____	_____	_____	_____
K.	**Financial FTE Enrollment change from previous year:**			_____%	_____%	_____%	_____%	_____%	_____%
L.	**FTE students (fall)**	(50*)	_____	_____	_____	_____	_____	_____	_____
M.	**Tuition Discount Factor (J divided by L):**		_____	_____	_____	_____	_____	_____	_____

*Refers to corresponding item on worksheet in chapter 3, "User Data."

Median Values for Similar Institutions

FTE ≤ 1500, from Liberal Arts Colleges II

	1976	1977	1978	1979	1980	1981	1982
Change in Constant (1971) Dollar Net Student Revenue (20 institutions)**		−7.1%	4.6%	4.8%			
Change in Constant (1971) Dollar Tuition Rate (20 institutions)		3.1%	−0.2%	0.7%			
Change in Financial FTE Enrollments (20 institutions)		−2.4%	8.6%	−6.5%			
Tuition Discount Factor (20 institutions)	1.16	1.18	1.19	1.16			

**Less restricted and unrestricted scholarships and fellowships.

Source: W. John Minter and Howard R. Bowen, *Independent Higher Education: Fifth Annual Report on Financial and Educational Trends in the Independent Sector of American Higher Education,* Washington, D.C., National Institute of Independent Colleges and Universities, 1980.

Explanation of Calculations

Unrestricted (or "unfunded") student aid is deducted because it represents a tuition discount. By deducting such aid, the true net revenue received from students is shown.

Dividing the net figure by the Higher Education Price Index gives an indication of what this revenue can buy in constant dollars. Year-to-year growth of zero percent indicates the institution is keeping up with a rough measure of inflation.

The financial FTE is an imputed enrollment figure determined by dividing tuition revenue by the tuition rate (both in current dollars). Part-timers, full-timers, and summer enrollments are equated only according to their contribution to tuition revenue. Students with tuition waivers are not counted unless a bookkeeping entry crediting tuition revenue and charging an expense such as benefits is made. Financial FTE is the "business manager's enrollment," the equivalent number of full-time tuition payers. It is affected by an increased number of refunds, by changes in spring semester and summer enrollments, and by changes in tuition remissions. Thus, it is financially more useful than the fall enrollment count. The **Tuition Discount Factor** reflects the discrepancy between the financial FTE and fall FTE.

Interpretations

Declines in net student revenues. The causes of a decline can be determined by examining the other lines on the worksheet. Falling enrollments, subinflation tuition increases, or too much student aid may be involved. Subinflation tuition makes "catch-up" increases very difficult should an institution face a revenue crisis. Falling enrollments require a major analysis of the institution's recruiting and academic policies.

Level net student revenues. In this situation, student support of the institution is as high as at the beginning of the period.

Increasing net student revenues. Generally, this is associated with increasing enrollments. The institution should note whether tuition rate trends add to or detract from any increases in net student-derived revenue. When enrollment growth slows, many institutions must turn to larger tuition increases.

Limitations

Enrollment changes are caused by many factors, one of which is tuition price. Most college administrators realize, however, that changes in institutional reputation or college-going preferences may be more telling.

Merely keeping up with the national college and university inflation index may be insufficient to keep the institution financially sound. Local inflation may be higher, or the institution may find that other sources of revenue do not grow at the rate of budgetary inflation.

Further Analysis

Enrollment changes may be further analyzed by examining "market share" changes over time. The institutions may wish to measure its freshman class as a proportion of the total of its 10 closest competitors' freshman classes. The institution may thus determine if it is losing ground against competitors or if it is merely the victim of declining numbers of potential students. Losses to competition call for a strong program to differentiate the institution. A decline in the number of available students, however, means the institution should consider reducing programs or attracting new types of students.

It may be necessary to examine unrestricted aid policies. Are all "unmet needs" met by the institution? Is more aid than necessary being given in order to stimulate enrollment? Has some dollar amount been fixed as the limit of financial aid awarded from unrestricted funds? These policies may have been altered in the last five years and may be responsible for some of the changes noted above.

Another measure of the adequacy of tuition revenue trends warrants attention. The ratio of tuition revenue to instruction expenditure shows the tuition-supported proportion of expenditure that is applied to the direct education of the student. In effect, changes in instruction expenditures are compared with tuition revenues.

Calculation Worksheet (supplement)

Fiscal year ending:	1976	1977	1978	1979	1980	1981	1982
N. Instruction expenditure (13*)	$____	$____	$____	$____	$____	$____	$____
O. **Tuition revenue to instruction expenditure ratio (C divided by N):**	____	____	____	____	____	____	____

* Refers to corresponding item on worksheet in chapter 3, "User Data."

Category: **Changes Affecting Financial Resources**
Selected Statistic:
Government-Derived Inflow Proportion

Significance of Statistic

Shifts in this proportion may indicate major changes in the revenue strategy of the institution and an increase in risk. Growing dependence on government funds may be the only reasonable way for the institution to proceed, given that government student aid programs have undergone major changes. The institution should know how these shifts affect its own programs, however. Most government funds require greater administration, accountability, and reporting than unrestricted tuition revenue. This shift of revenue can contribute to shifts in the overall character of the institution. Increases in government-derived revenue show that the institution acknowledges the goals advanced in Congress' higher education funding legislation. The institution's mission may shift if its priorities differ from legislated goals.

Calculation Worksheet

	Fiscal year ending:	1976	1977	1978	1979	1980	1981	1982
A.	Government appropriations (federal, state, local) (2*)	$____	$____	$____	$____	$____	$____	$____
B.	Government grants and contracts (federal, state, and local, including scholarship aid, work-study revenues, research funds, education "title" funds, etc.) (3*)	$____	$____	$____	$____	$____	$____	$____
C.	All government student aid *not included* in revenues listed in A and B above (56*)	$____	$____	$____	$____	$____	$____	$____
D.	Total government inflows (A plus B plus C)	$____	$____	$____	$____	$____	$____	$____
E.	Total current fund revenues (9*)	$____	$____	$____	$____	$____	$____	$____
F.	**Proportion of current fund revenues paid (directly or indirectly) by government sources (D divided by E):**	____	____	____	____	____	____	____

* Refers to corresponding item on worksheet in chapter 3, "User Data."

Median Values for Similar Institutions: Not available.

Explanation of Calculations

Some funds from government sources, such as BEOGs, which do not flow directly through the institution's current funds, are treated as a tuition revenue replacement and have been included. Other government-derived revenue such as veterans benefits could have been treated similarly, but figures are not always available.

Dividing by current fund revenues gives the proportion of current fund support, including auxiliaries, that originates with the government.

Interpretations

Increasing dependence on government-derived revenue. Increasing dependence implies that government revenues are replacing other revenues or that government revenues are supplementing other revenues (or both). If government revenue is replacing other forms of revenue, the institution should identify those constituents that are reducing support. Are gift revenues declining? Are funds from parents and students failing to match overall growth? If government-derived revenues are supplementing other forms of income, the institution should determine if new programs, or program expansions made possible by the additional government funds, are consistent with the planned direction of the institution.

Limitations

Some scholarship aid does not go to the institution but must be used by students to pay off-campus expenses. To that extent, the ratio is partially inflated.

Several forms of indirect dependence on government, including tax advantages, social security, and veterans benefits, have not been included.

Further Analysis

State, federal, and local revenue sources may be calculated separately to identify the government sector in which the largest increases have occurred.

Student aid (need-based or otherwise), unrestricted funds, and program funds are areas that may further explain changes in dependence.

Category: **Changes Affecting Financial Resources**
Selected Statistic: **Revenue Bar Graphs**

Significance of Statistic

Changes in the proportion of support from various sources can be used to find both strengths and weaknesses in an institution's revenue strategy. Of greatest concern are declines in the proportion of revenue from gifts and marked increases in the proportion of revenue from tuition. Institutions that become more heavily dependent on tuition revenues are offering students less for their money. In this situation the added benefits brought by other sources of revenue may be declining.

Calculation Worksheet

Values needed to fill in the bar graphs can be calculated on the following worksheet.

	Fiscal year ending:		1976	1977	1978	1979	1980	1981	1982
A.	Tuition and fees	(1*)	$_____	$_____	$_____	$_____	$_____	$_____	$_____
B.	Government appropriations (federal, state, and local)	(2*)	$_____	$_____	$_____	$_____	$_____	$_____	$_____
C.	Government grants and contracts	(3*)	$_____	$_____	$_____	$_____	$_____	$_____	$_____
D.	Private gifts, grants, and contracts	(4*)	$_____	$_____	$_____	$_____	$_____	$_____	$_____
E.	Endowment income	(5*)	$_____	$_____	$_____	$_____	$_____	$_____	$_____
F.	Other current fund revenues	(6*)	$_____	$_____	$_____	$_____	$_____	$_____	$_____
G.	E&G + MT	(23*)	$_____	$_____	$_____	$_____	$_____	$_____	$_____

* Refers to corresponding item on worksheet in chapter 3, "User Data."

Proportions

		1976	1977	1978	1979	1980	1981	1982
H.	**Tuition (A divided by G):**	_____	_____	_____	_____	_____	_____	_____
I.	**Appropriations (B divided by G):**	_____	_____	_____	_____	_____	_____	_____
J.	**Grants and contracts (C divided by G):**	_____	_____	_____	_____	_____	_____	_____
K.	**Private gifts (D divided by G):**	_____	_____	_____	_____	_____	_____	_____
L.	**Endowment income (E divided by G):**	_____	_____	_____	_____	_____	_____	_____
M.	**Other revenue (F divided by G):**	_____	_____	_____	_____	_____	_____	_____

Revenue Proportions for Five Years

Instructions: For each year in each category, draw a line indicating the percentage of total revenues.

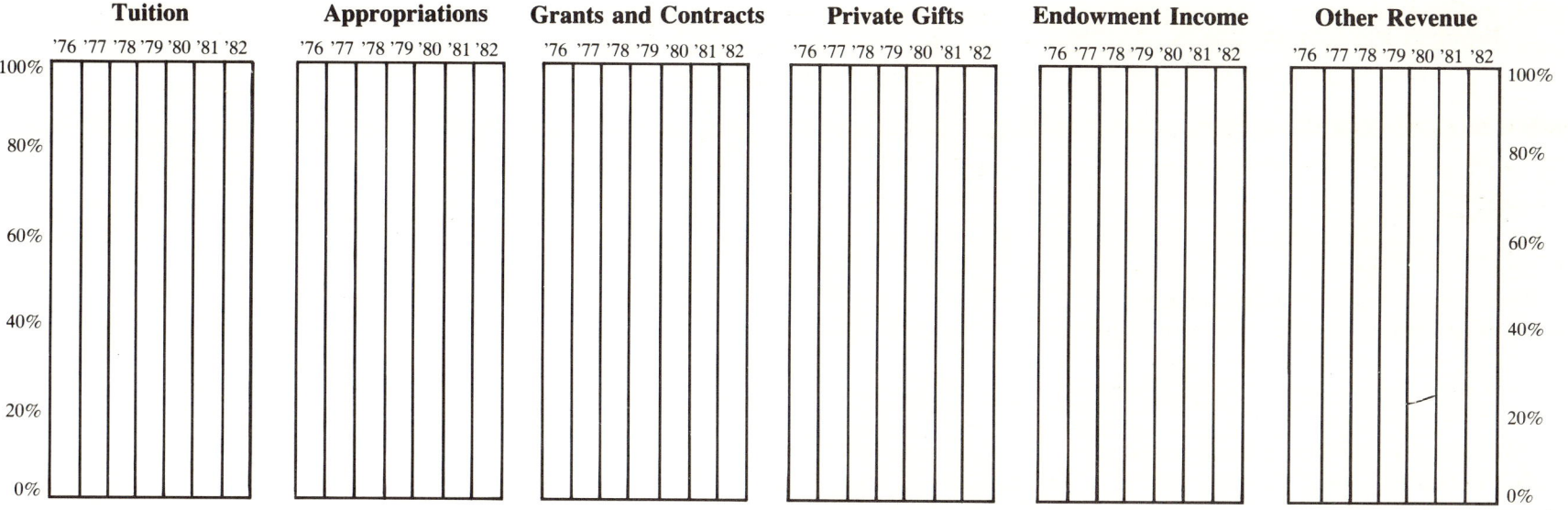

Median Values for Similar Institutions

FTE ≤ 1500, from Liberal Arts Colleges II

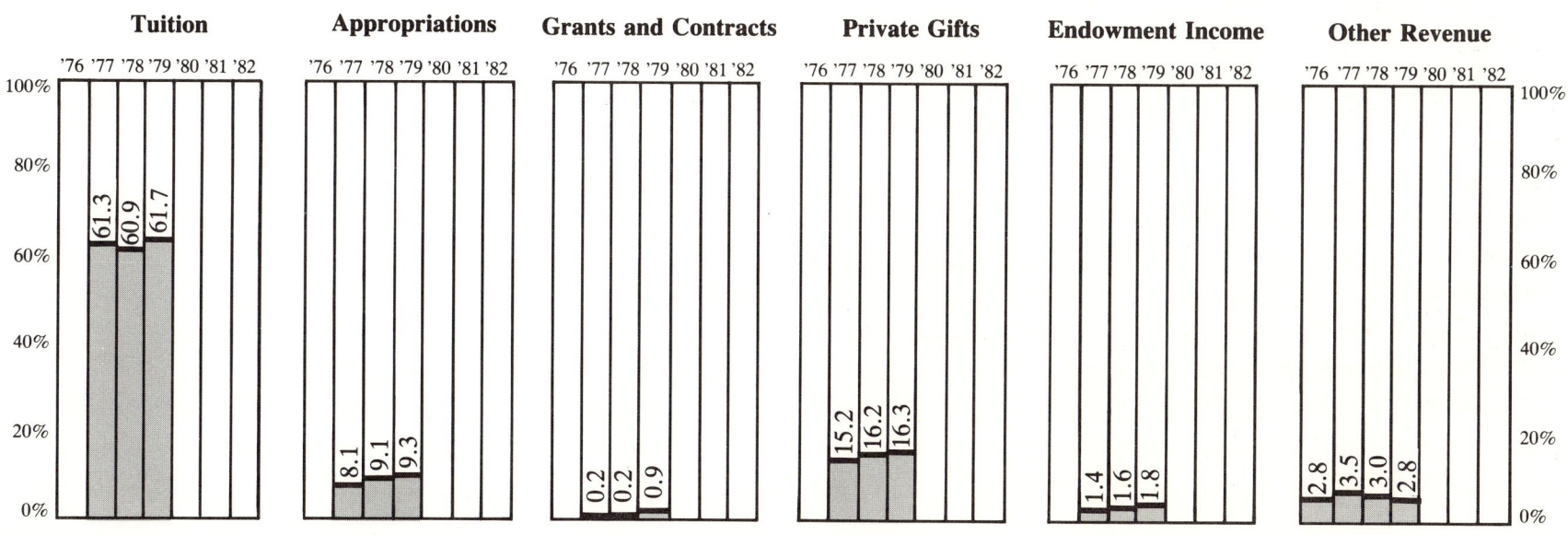

Source: Audited financial statements coded to NACUBO standards, John Minter Associates, Boulder, Colorado.

Explanation of Calculations

The revenue categories were chosen because of their availability in annual financial reports.

By dividing by educational and general expenditures and mandatory transfers, the college can measure the proportion of expenditure support given by each revenue category.

Interpretations

Increasing tuition dependence. Students are paying a larger portion of the costs of education. However, if dependence on government is increasing as well, the net increase to students and parents may be negligible.

Decreasing gift dependence. Fund raising is not keeping up with the overall growth of the budget.

Decreasing endowment income growth. There are many potential factors here. See the **Endowment Ratio** in the "Financial Resources" section for further analysis.

Limitations

Changes in revenue dependence are not necessarily positive or negative. They do reflect shifting revenue strategies, intended or unintended, and are worthy of investigation.

Further Analysis

An interesting set of deeper analyses involves the gift revenue proportions. Several important pieces of information showing historical trends should be gathered:

- What proportion of alumni contribute?
- What is the average gift?
- What is the breakdown among alumni, foundation, corporate, and other gifts?
- What was spent on fund raising?
- What was the cost of each dollar raised?

Category: Changes Affecting Financial Resources
Selected Statistic: Contributed Services Ratio

Significance of Statistic

The extra "education value" that a church-related institution can offer is often partially provided by the contributed services of religious personnel. The financial value of these services is one measure of the sponsoring religious body's commitment to the mission of the institution. Services contributed by religious personnel allow the institution to provide distinctive services at lower cost to students.

Calculation Worksheet

	Fiscal year ending:	1976	1977	1978	1979	1980	1981	1982
A.	Market value of services provided by religious personnel	$_____	$_____	$_____	$_____	$_____	$_____	$_____
B.	Actual cash payments for services of religious personnel	$_____	$_____	$_____	$_____	$_____	$_____	$_____
C.	Value of contributed services (including gifts and other types). (A minus B) (Some institutions may wish to fill out this line directly, omitting A and B.) (10*)	$_____	$_____	$_____	$_____	$_____	$_____	$_____
D.	E&G + MT (23*)	$_____	$_____	$_____	$_____	$_____	$_____	$_____
E.	**Contributed Services Ratio (C divided by D):**	_____	_____	_____	_____	_____	_____	_____

* Refers to corresponding item on worksheet in chapter 3, "User Data."

Median Values for Similar Institutions: Not Available

Explanation of Calculations

In many institutions the value of contributed services is available directly from financial statements as part of the gifts revenue item.

Dividing by total expenditures measures the budget proportion supported by contributed services.

Interpretations

Declines in the proportion of support. Both the character and the financial base of the institution are changing. The religious "presence" may be declining as an important basis of the institution's financial stability.

Level proportional support. Although this trend does not have the strongly negative connotations of a proportional decline, some further analysis may be necessary to determine the potential for decline. Many sponsoring religious organizations do not have a steady flow of new personnel. As the age of contributing personnel increases, the potential for sharp declines in this source of support increases.

Growing proportional support. Strength in this area is indicated.

Limitations

To the extent that the presence of religious personnel in academic, administrative, and support service positions is perceived as integral to the mission and identity of the institution, the ratio may understate their value in attracting students and external gifts. To the extent that religious personnel are seen as less than fully qualified for the positions they hold, the opposite may be true.

Further Analysis

The average age of contributing religious personnel can be estimated and shown as a trend.

Category: **Changes Affecting Financial Resources**
Selected Statistic: **Expenditures per Student**

Significance of Statistic

Trends in spending per student can indicate problems with budget control and changes in efficiency. Large increases may indicate an inability to adjust expenditures to changes in the size of the student body. Unless revenues increase as fast on a per student basis, the institution will lose resources.

Calculation Worksheet

	Fiscal year ending:	1976	1977	1978	1979	1980	1981	1982
A.	E&G + MT (23*)	$_____	$_____	$_____	$_____	$_____	$_____	$_____
B.	FTE students (fall) (50*)	_____	_____	_____	_____	_____	_____	_____
C.	Expenditures per student (A divided by B)	$_____	$_____	$_____	$_____	$_____	$_____	$_____
D.	Higher Education Price Index (1971 = 1.00)	1.379	1.468	1.567	1.689	1.856	_____	_____
E.	Expenditures per Student in Constant (1971) Dollars (C divided by D)	$_____	$_____	$_____	$_____	$_____	$_____	$_____
F.	Change from previous year:		_____%	_____%	_____%	_____%	_____%	_____%

* Refers to corresponding item on worksheet in chapter 3, "User Data."

Median Values for Similar Institutions

FTE ≤ 1500, from Liberal Arts Colleges II

	1976	1977	1978	1979	1980	1981	1982
E&G expenditures per FTE student** (28 institutions)	$2447.50	$2825.50	$3013.50	$3037.50			
E&G expenditures per FTE student (28 institutions)	$2990.00	$3401.50	$3450.80	$3940.00			
E&G expenditures per student in Constant (1971) Dollars (27 institutions)	$2168.30	$2317.10	$2202.20	$2332.80			

**Less restricted and unrestricted scholarships and fellowships.
Source: Audited financial statements coded to NACUBO standards, John Minter Associates, Boulder, Colorado.

Explanation of Calculations

Educational and general expenditures are used to indicate the cost of services provided to students.

Interpretations

Declining constant dollar values. Possible interpretations are that the institution is gaining efficiency because of rising enrollment or that it has chosen to provide fewer services to the student.

Increasing constant dollar values. Once again, several interpretations are possible: there has been a decrease in efficiency due to enrollment declines; the institution's revenue-raising capability is staying ahead of inflation; the institution has chosen to provide more services, funded or unfunded, to the student; or the institution's actual inflation rate exceeds the nationally computed rate.

Limitations

Large fluctuations may indicate two problems worthy of further analysis (the statistic does not separate them): budgetary response to enrollment change may be poor, or enrollment is out of control.

Educational and general expenditures do not adequately measure total services available to students.

Comparability among institutions is very limited given the varying effect of inflation on different institutions and the range of program offerings, administrative styles, and other services offered.

Further Analysis

Much of the extra analysis, including **Student to Faculty Ratios** and programs offered, was presented in the "Nonfinancial Resources" section.

Category: **Changes Affecting Financial Resources**
Selected Statistic:
Expenditures—Unit Trends

Significance of the Statistic

The wage or price indexes of several major components of the budget are presented to facilitate analysis of expenditure trends. By comparing institutional "line-item" expenditure increases with national trends, the institution may be able to gauge its own effort in the area of cost control or cost expansion. Expenditure areas of greatest cost pressure or conservation are highlighted by this analysis.

Calculation Worksheet

	Fiscal year ending:	1976	1977	1978	1979	1980	1981	1982
Exempt Staff Salaries								
A.	Average exempt staff salaries (administrative and institutional services) (26*)	$_____	$_____	$_____	$_____	$_____	$_____	$_____
B.	Exempt staff salary index (1971 = 1.00)**	1.268	1.327	1.389	1.486	1.598	_____	_____
C.	Exempt staff salaries deflated by index (A divided by B)	$_____	$_____	$_____	$_____	$_____	$_____	$_____
D.	**Change from previous year:**		_____%	_____%	_____%	_____%	_____%	_____%
Books and Periodicals								
E.	Total books and periodicals expenditures (28*)	$_____	$_____	$_____	$_____	$_____	$_____	$_____
F.	Books and periodicals index (1971 = 1.00)**	1.739	1.849	1.978	2.183	2.512	_____	_____
G.	Books and periodicals deflated by index (E divided by F)	$_____	$_____	$_____	$_____	$_____	$_____	$_____
H.	**Change from previous year (index is a weighted average of subindexes for U.S. hardcover books (55%), U.S. periodicals (30%), and foreign monographs (15%)):**		_____%	_____%	_____%	_____%	_____%	_____%

* Refers to corresponding item on worksheet in chapter 3, "User Data."
** D. Kent Halstead, "Higher Education Prices and Price Indexes: 1980 Update," *Business Officer*, Washington, D.C., NACUBO, October 1980, p. 18.

	Fiscal year ending:	1976	1977	1978	1979	1980	1981	1982
Utilities								
I.	Utilities included in operation and maintenance of plant (24*)	$_____	$_____	$_____	$_____	$_____	$_____	$_____
J.	Utilities index (1971 = 1.00)**	1.912	2.252	2.552	2.799	3.569	_____	_____
K.	Utilities deflated by index (I divided by J)	$_____	$_____	$_____	$_____	$_____	$_____	$_____
L.	**Change from previous year (index is a weighted average of subindexes for heating fuel (30%), commercial power (60%), and water and sewage (10%)):**	_____%	_____%	_____%	_____%	_____%	_____%	_____%

*Refers to corresponding item on worksheet in chapter 3, "User Data."
**D. Kent Halstead, "Higher Education Prices and Price Indexes: 1980 Update," *Business Officer*, Washington, D.C., NACUBO, October 1980, p. 18.

Explanation of Calculations

The annual percentages will be zero if the institution has maintained the scope of its operation, has experienced inflation near the national average, and has the same composition of expenditures in each subgroup as in the national indexes.

Interpretations

Variances from national growth rates may be caused by either consumption shifts or price changes at rates different from the national average. If the institution uses less electricity or purchases fewer books, the calculated growth rate would tend to be below zero. If, however, the institution has experienced electricity rate hikes or book price increases above the national average, deviation from the national average would tend to be above zero.

Variances from national averages should partially reflect budget priorities at the institution. This information should contain nothing unexpected if the institution understands the cost pressures it faces and the actions it has taken to minimize the effect of inflation.

Limitations

It is very difficult to separate local inflation variances from consumption changes.

These indexes are intended only as a general approximation of inflation in a few categories of expenditures.

Interpretation of the figures is limited to amplifying current expenditure strategies and assisting forecasting. Very little can be inferred about the "health" of the organization from these trends. They are included only to provide another piece of financial information that may be helpful to policy makers.

Further Analysis

NACUBO's *Business Officer* (October 1980) contains several sets of subindexes, such as salaries for library personnel. The institution may wish to refine its analysis of one or more of these areas by breaking the expenditures into subcategories.

Utilities may be separated into consumption factors and a price per unit of consumption factors. The national indexes assume constant consumption. Thus, total dollars spent for utilities may be less useful as a basis of analysis than separate comparisons of consumption and unit cost with the national trends. Also, the cost per volume of library acquisition and the increase in total volumes acquired are separable factors and may be analyzed in terms of volume and unit price changes.

Category: **Changes Affecting Financial Resources**

Selected Statistic: **Expenditure Bar Graphs**

Significance of Statistic

Major changes in the expenditure allocation strategies of the institution are revealed in the following bar graphs. Most of the areas listed are functional categories. Thus, declines or increases in the proportion spent on any area indicate changes in institutional priority for that function. If the proportion spent on instruction has declined, for example, this analysis will show which areas have increased proportionately.

Calculation Worksheet

The values needed to fill in the bar graphs can be calculated on the following worksheet.

	Fiscal year ending:	1976	1977	1978	1979	1980	1981	1982
A.	Instruction (13*)	$____	$____	$____	$____	$____	$____	$____
B.	Research (14*)	$____	$____	$____	$____	$____	$____	$____
C.	Public service (15*)	$____	$____	$____	$____	$____	$____	$____
D.	Academic support (16*)	$____	$____	$____	$____	$____	$____	$____
E.	Student services (17*)	$____	$____	$____	$____	$____	$____	$____
F.	Institutional support (18*)	$____	$____	$____	$____	$____	$____	$____
G.	Operation and maintenance of plant (19*)	$____	$____	$____	$____	$____	$____	$____
H.	Scholarships and fellowships from unrestricted funds (20*)	$____	$____	$____	$____	$____	$____	$____
I.	Mandatory transfers (22*)	$____	$____	$____	$____	$____	$____	$____
J.	Total E&G expenditures (excluding restricted student aid) (add A through I)	$____	$____	$____	$____	$____	$____	$____

*Refers to corresponding item on worksheet in chapter 3, "User Data."

Proportions

		1976	1977	1978	1979	1980	1981	1982
K.	Instruction (A divided by J):	____	____	____	____	____	____	____
L.	Research (B divided by J):	____	____	____	____	____	____	____
M.	Public service (C divided by J):	____	____	____	____	____	____	____
N.	Academic support (D divided by J):	____	____	____	____	____	____	____
O.	Student services (E divided by J):	____	____	____	____	____	____	____
P.	Institutional support (F divided by J):	____	____	____	____	____	____	____
Q.	Operation and maintenance of plant (G divided by J):	____	____	____	____	____	____	____
R.	Unrestricted student aid (H divided by J):	____	____	____	____	____	____	____
S.	Mandatory transfers (I divided by J):	____	____	____	____	____	____	____

Expenditure Proportions for Five Years

Instructions: For each year in each category, draw a line indicating the percentage of total expenditures.

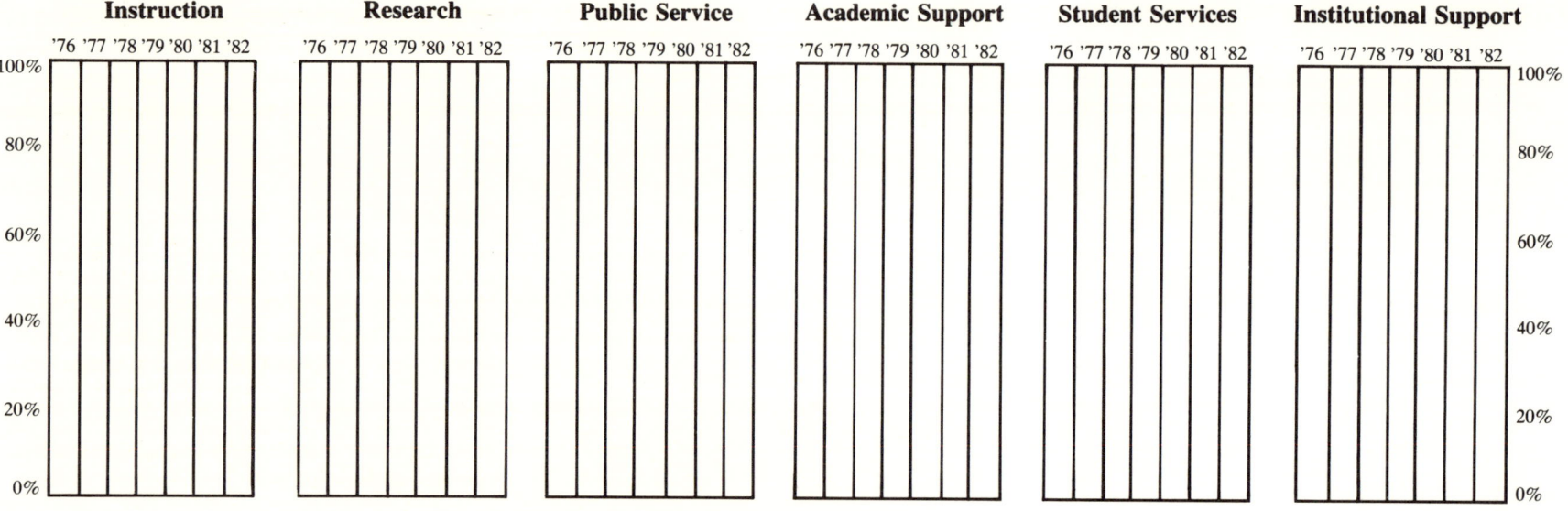

Median Values for Similar Institutions

FTE ≤ 1500, from Liberal Arts Colleges II

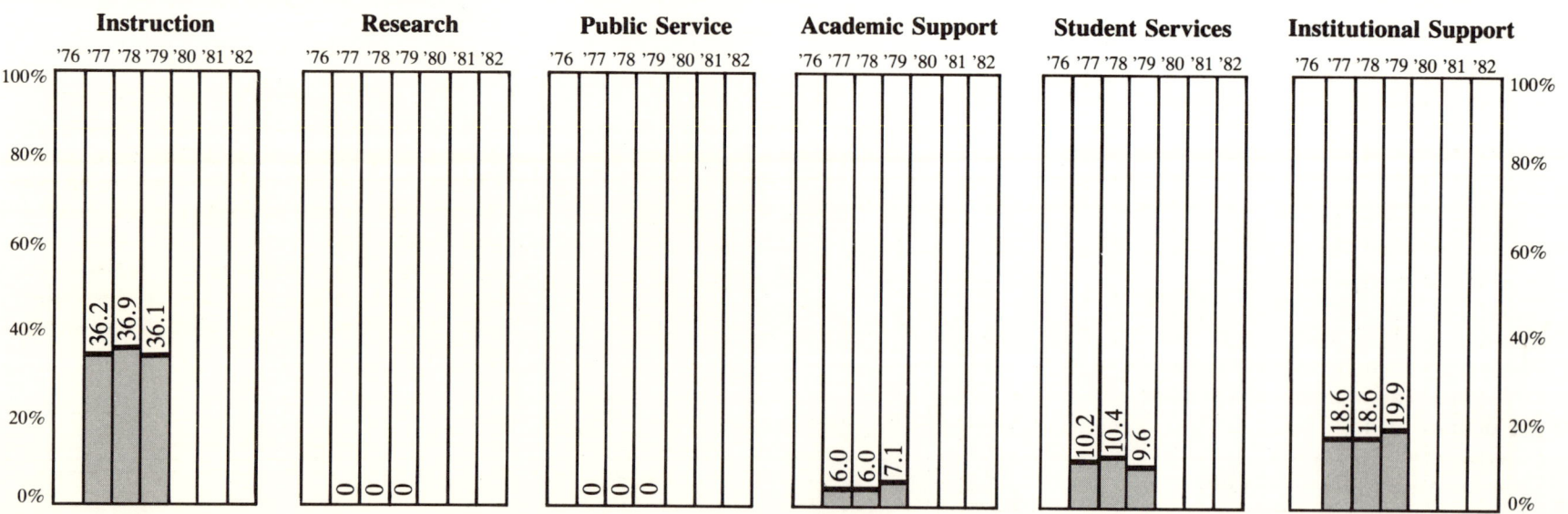

Source: Audited financial statements coded to NACUBO standards, John Minter Associates, Boulder, Colorado.

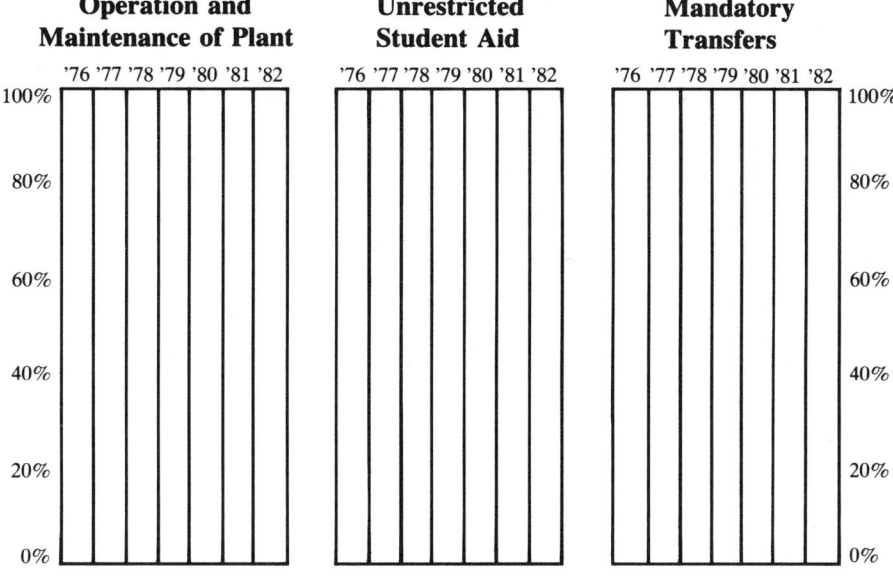

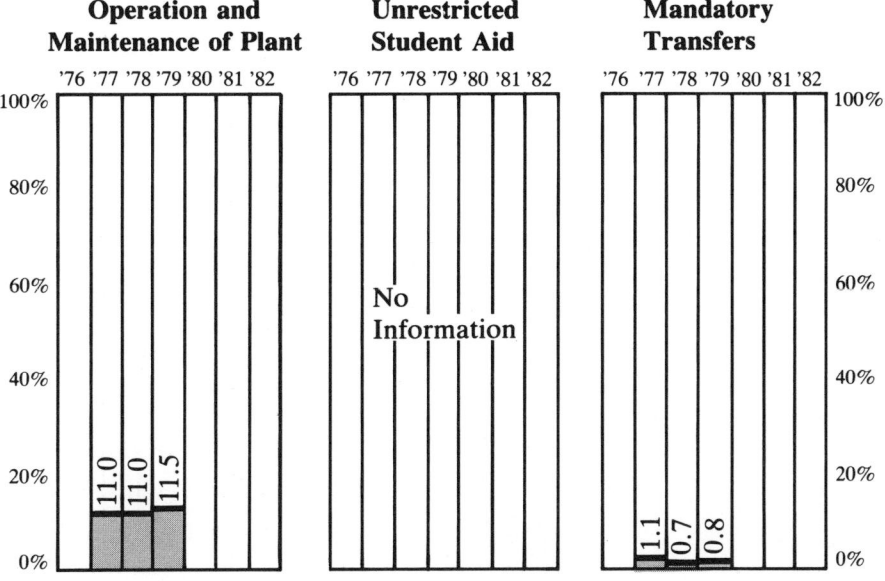

Explanation of Calculations

All expenditures and mandatory transfers in the current fund, except restricted scholarships and fellowships, are included in computing the base. Restricted scholarships and fellowships such as SEOGs were excluded because of the distortion that may be caused when outside agencies provide student aid through the current fund.

Interpretations

The bar graphs show how changes in the instruction budget may be affected by budget changes in other areas. Changes in the **Instruction Proportion** may be caused by additional library expenditures or academic support, utilities costs as part of plant operation and maintenance, increased debt costs as part of mandatory transfers, or increased student services expenditures.

Limitations

The "condition" of the institution is not revealed by these graphs. They can show only expenditure patterns during the five years.

Further Analysis

The budget proportion allotted to specific items such as utilities, library acquisitions, and financial aid administration may be analyzed. More detailed items within an area represented by one of the bar graphs may also be charted.

Expenditure factors such as salaries or contracted services can be analyzed to determine if the institution has changed its method of delivering services.

Appendix A Self-Assessment Indicators and Calculations

Financial Resources: Indicators and Calculations

 A. Short-term—Unrestricted Current Fund Ratio

  Calculation: $\dfrac{\text{Unrestricted current fund assets}}{\text{Unrestricted current fund liabilities}}$

 B. Intermediate-term—Available Funds Ratio*

  Calculation: $\dfrac{\text{Unrestricted current fund balance plus quasi-endowment market value}}{\text{Educational and general expenditures plus mandatory transfers (E\&G + MT)}}$

 C. Long-term—Endowment Ratio

  Calculation: $\dfrac{\text{Endowment market value}}{\text{E\&G + MT}}$

Hidden Financial Resources (estimated only):

 D. Value of Marketable Land Ratio

  Calculation: $\dfrac{\text{Value of marketable land}}{\text{E\&G + MT}}$

 E. Financial Support from Affiliated Organizations or Patron Foundations

  Calculation: $\dfrac{\text{Financial support from affiliated organizations or patron foundations}}{\text{E\&G + MT}}$

*Core Statistic

Flexibility: Indicators and Calculations

A. Debt Service to Revenue Ratio

Calculation: $$\frac{\text{Debt service due}}{\text{Current fund revenues}}$$

B. Acceptance Rate*

Calculation: $$\frac{\text{Acceptances of freshman and transfer applicants}}{\text{Freshman and transfer applications}}$$

or

$$\frac{\text{Acceptances of freshman and transfer applicants}}{\text{Inquiries}}$$

C. Tenured Faculty Ratio

Calculation: $$\frac{\text{Number of tenured faculty or faculty with long-term contracts (greater than five years)}}{\text{FTE faculty (fall)}}$$

Nonfinancial Resources: Indicators and Calculations

A. Student Characteristics

1. Average test scores of entering freshmen
2. Selectivity (same as **Acceptance Rate**)
3. Percentage of entering students from top 20% of high school class
4. Percentage of entering students from top 40% of high school class

B. Institutional Attraction

1. Yield Rate

    Calculation: $$\frac{\text{New students (freshmen and transfers)}}{\text{Acceptances of freshmen and transfer applicants}}$$

2. Retention:

    Calculation: Percentage of previous year's eligible students who enroll for next class

3. Student Services Expenditures per Student

    Calculation: $$\frac{\text{Student services expenditures**}}{\text{Total student headcount (fall)}}$$

*Core Statistic
**Deflated by Higher Education Price Index (HEPI): 1971=1.00

C. **Academic Program**

  1. Instruction Proportion*

   Calculation: $$\frac{\text{Instruction expenditures}}{\text{E\&G + MT minus restricted fund scholarships}}$$

  2. Instruction per FTE Student*

   Calculation: $$\frac{\text{Instruction expenditures**}}{\text{FTE students (fall)}}$$

D. **Faculty**

  1. Change in Average Compensation*

   Calculation: Average full-time faculty compensation***

  2. Student to Faculty Ratio*

   Calculation: $$\frac{\text{FTE students}}{\text{FTE faculty}}$$

E. **Staff**

   Calculation: $$\frac{\text{Total student headcount (fall)}}{\text{FTE administrative exempt staff (excluding auxiliary staff)}}$$

F. **Deferred Physical Plant Maintenance**

   Calculation: $$\frac{\text{Estimate of deferred physical plant maintenance}}{\text{E\&G + MT}}$$

Changes Affecting Financial Resources: Indicators and Calculations

  A. **Student-Derived Revenue Trends**

  1. Constant (1971) Dollar Net Student Revenue*

   Calculation: Tuition and fees minus scholarships and fellowships from unrestricted funds**

  2. Constant (1971) Dollar Tuition Rate*/**

  3. Financial FTE Enrollments*

   Calculation: $$\frac{\text{Net student revenue}}{\text{Tuition and fee rate per year for a full-time student}}$$

  4. Tuition Discount Factor*

   Calculation: $$\frac{\text{Financial FTE enrollments}}{\text{FTE students}}$$

*Core Statistic
**Deflated by Higher Education Price Index (HEPI): 1971=1.00
***Deflated by Consumer Price Index (CPI): 1971=1.00

B. **Government-Derived Inflow Proportion**

 Calculation: $\dfrac{\text{Total government-related inflows}}{\text{Current fund revenues}}$

C. **Revenue Bar Graphs**
- Tuition and fees
- Appropriations
- Grants and contracts
- Gifts
- Endowment income
- Other revenues

D. **Contributed Services Ratio**

 Calculation: $\dfrac{\text{Value of contributed services}}{\text{E\&G + MT}}$

E. **Expenditures per Student**

 Calculation: $\dfrac{\text{E\&G+MT minus scholarships and fellowships from restricted funds**}}{\text{FTE students (fall)}}$

F. **Expenditures—Unit Trends**
- Average exempt staff salaries
- Books and periodicals
- Utilities

G. **Expenditure Bar Graphs**
- Instruction
- Research
- Public service
- Academic support
- Student services
- Institutional support
- Operation and maintenance of plant
- Scholarships and fellowships (unrestricted only)
- Mandatory transfers

**Deflated by Higher Education Price Index (HEPI): 1971=1.00

Appendix B Glossary

> Most of the following are explained in greater detail in the third edition of NACUBO's *College and University Business Administration*. The numbers in parentheses refer to the appropriate part and chapter of that volume.

ACADEMIC SUPPORT. Academic administration and personnel development; audiovisual services, computing services, course and curriculum development, demonstration schools, libraries, museums and galleries. (5:2)

ASSETS (CURRENT FUND). Cash, accounts receivable, notes receivable, investments, amounts due from other fund groups. (5:2)

AUXILIARY ENTERPRISES. Enterprises managed as essentially self-supporting, including residence halls, food services, and bookstores. (5:2)

CONSUMER PRICE INDEX (CPI). Change in cost of typical wage-earner purchases of goods and services expressed as a percentage of the cost of these same goods and services in the same base year. For the *Financial Self-Assessment* workbook, the base year is 1971=1.00.

CONTRIBUTED SERVICES. Monetary value of services donated by the sponsoring religious group. (5:1)

CURRENT FUND. Resources to be used for current operating purposes. (5:2)

CURRENT FUND BALANCE. Includes allocations by operating management, budget balances brought forward from prior fiscal periods, and the unallocated balance. (5:2)

CURRENT FUND REVENUES. All unrestricted gifts, grants, and other resources earned during the reporting period, and restricted resources to the extent that such funds were expended. (5:2)

DEBT SERVICE PAYMENTS. Principal, interest, and sinking fund payments. (5:4)

ENDOWMENT INCOME. Unrestricted income from endowment and similar funds, restricted income from endowment and similar funds expended for current operations, and income from funds held by others under irrevocable trusts. (5:2)

EXEMPT EMPLOYEE. One whose conditions of employment and compensation are not subject to the provisions of the Fair Labor Standards Act as amended. Exempt employees are not eligible for overtime payment. According to Section 13 of the act, an exempt employee is "any employee employed in a bona fide executive, administrative, or professional capacity...."*

FACULTY COMPENSATION. Salary plus benefits. (2:8)

GOVERNMENT APPROPRIATIONS. All unrestricted amounts received or made available to an institution by legislative acts or local taxing authority, and restricted amounts from those same sources that are expended for current operations. (5:2)

GOVERNMENT GRANTS AND CONTRACTS. All unrestricted amounts received or made available by grants and contracts from government agencies and all amounts received or made available through restricted grants and contracts to the extent expended for current operations. (5:2)

HIGHER EDUCATION PRICE INDEX (HEPI). Index of goods and services purchased by colleges and universities for their operations (education and general current operations). HEPI includes faculty funding and research, administration, secretarial and clerical services, fringe benefits, supplies and materials, equipment, utilities, books, communications, and data processing. In calculating the index, price changes for the items are averaged with weights that represent their relative importance in the spending of all higher education institutions. For the *Financial Self-Assessment* workbook, index numbers are computed on the base year 1971=1.00.

INDEPENDENT OPERATIONS. Expenditures and transfers for independent endeavors that may enhance the primary missions of the institution. (5:2)

INSTITUTIONAL SUPPORT. Central executive-level activities concerned with management and long-range planning and carried out by the governing board or chief executive, academic, or business officers; fiscal operations; administrative data processing; space management, staff personnel, and records; logistical activities that provide procurement, safety, security, or transportation; faculty and staff support services that are not operated as auxiliary enterprises; and community and alumni relations. (5:2)

INSTRUCTION. General academic instruction, occupational and vocational instruction, special session instruction, and community education. (5:2)

LIABILITIES (CURRENT FUND). Accounts and notes payable, accrued liabilities, deposits, amounts due to other fund groups, and deferred credits. (5:2)

LIBERAL ARTS COLLEGES II. Specific subset of institutions, eleven public and 449 private. These institutions may be termed "single-purpose" and are primarily liberal arts and teacher preparatory; they do not award doctorates and offer master's degrees only on a limited basis.

MANDATORY TRANSFERS. Legally binding transfers of restricted or unrestricted funds from the current funds group to other funds for the financing of the educational plant; grants agreements with the federal government, donors, or others to match gifts and grants to loan and other funds. (5:2)

OPERATION AND MAINTENANCE OF PLANT. Administration, custodial services, maintenance of buildings and grounds, utilities, trucking services, fire protection. Not included are expenditures from the institutional plant fund account. (5:2)

PRIVATE GIFTS, GRANTS, AND CONTRACTS. Amounts from nongovernment organizations and individuals. Includes all restricted and unrestricted gifts, grants, and bequests expended in the current fiscal year for current operations. (5:2)

PUBLIC SERVICE. Community and cooperative extension services, conferences and institutes, public lectures, radio, and television. (5:2)

QUASI-ENDOWMENT FUNDS (FUNDS FUNCTIONING AS ENDOWMENT). Funds that the governing board has decided to retain and invest. (5:3) (see also 4:1)

RESEARCH. Institutes and research centers; individual or project research. (5:2)

RESTRICTED FUNDS. Funds limited by donors and government agencies to specific purposes, programs, departments, or schools. (5:2)

SCHOLARSHIPS AND FELLOWSHIPS. Expenditures financed from current funds, restricted or unrestricted, and disbursed in the form of outright grants to students selected by the institution. (5:2) (see also 2:6)

STUDENT SERVICES. Admissions office, registrar, counseling and career guidance, financial aid administration. (5:2)

TUITION AND FEES. All tuition and fees assessed against students (net of refunds) for educational purposes. (5:2)

UNRESTRICTED FUNDS. All funds received for which no stipulation was made as to how they should be spent. (5:2)

A Glossary of Standard Terminology for Postsecondary Education, Boulder, Colorado, National Center for Higher Education Management Systems, 1977, p. 29.

Appendix C Retention of Entering Freshmen

The following graph shows how one institution tracked the freshman class for the years 1972 to 1978. The institution used the chart to update its five-year plan and to project enrollments for FY84–85.

	1972	1973	1974	1975	1976	1977	1978
To sophomore year	70.1%	74.7%	74.0%	71.2%	69.3%	74.7%	74.2%
To junior year	51.9%	54.3%	54.0%	52.9%	52.8%	57.2%	
To senior year	46.1%	48.7%	49.8%	50.8%	47.5%		

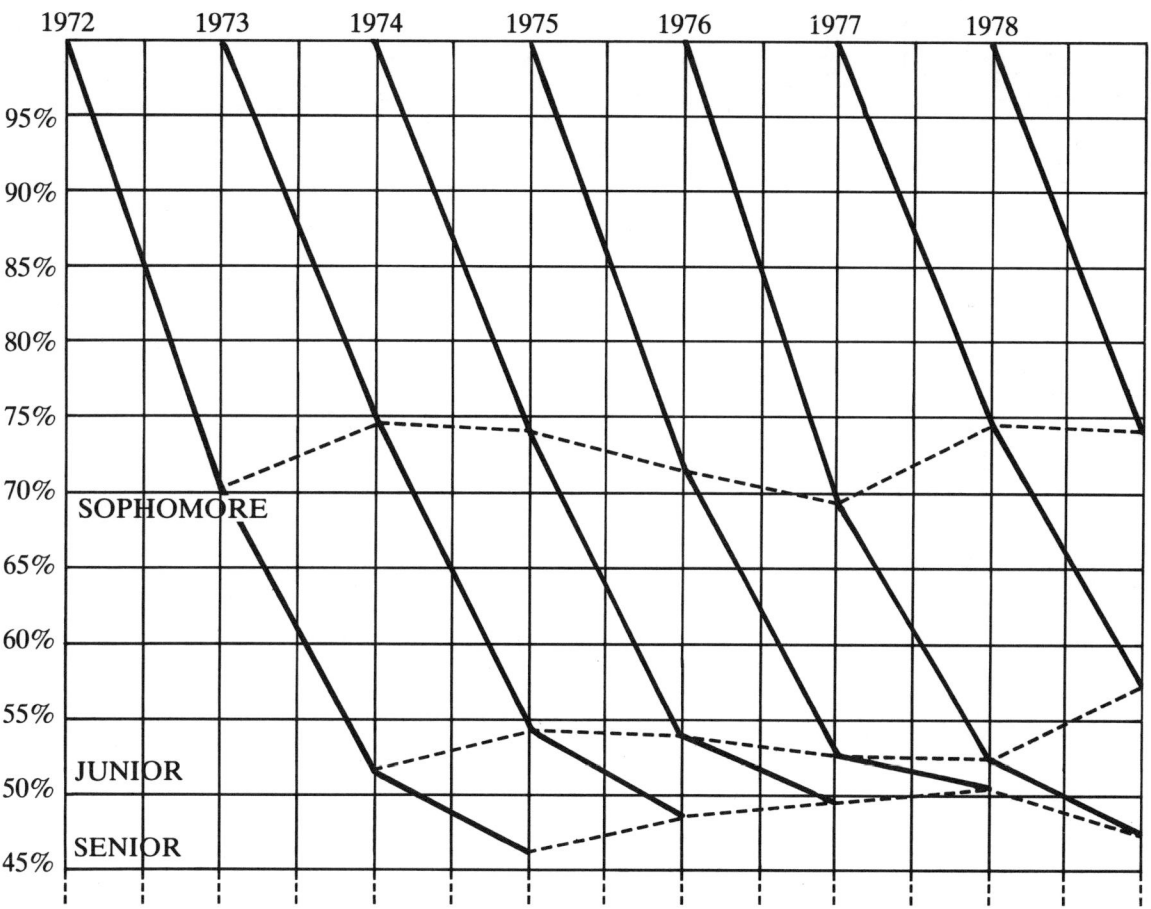

Courtesy Richard B. Jungkuntz, provost, Pacific Lutheran University.

Instructions: On the following chart list the number of freshmen, sophomores, juniors, and seniors for the years given. (Information can be gathered from admissions records.) When plotted on the blank graph on page 71, this information will show the percentages for each class. A comparison can also be made, for example, of the number and percentage of freshmen who returned in 1976 to the number and percentage of freshmen who returned in 1978. It is most important to use consistent information from year to year and to count the same type of students within the group defined as returning to the next class. Thus, accurate retention rates will be produced.

	Freshmen	Sophomores	Juniors	Seniors
1976:	_____	_____	_____	_____
% returning to next class		_____ %	_____ %	_____ %
1977:	_____	_____	_____	_____
% returning to next class		_____ %	_____ %	_____ %
1978:	_____	_____	_____	_____
% returning to next class		_____ %	_____ %	_____ %
1979:	_____	_____	_____	_____
% returning to next class		_____ %	_____ %	_____ %
1980:	_____	_____	_____	_____
% returning to next class		_____ %	_____ %	_____ %
1981:	_____	_____	_____	_____
% returning to next class		_____ %	_____ %	_____ %
1982:	_____	_____	_____	_____
% returning to next class		_____ %	_____ %	_____ %

Instructions: On the following graph plot the percentage of freshmen who returned as sophomores and again as juniors and seniors, beginning with the freshman class of 1976. Record the correct percentages to allow a visual understanding of the retention rate of entering freshmen. (The completed graph at the beginning of this section illustrates one method of plotting this information.)

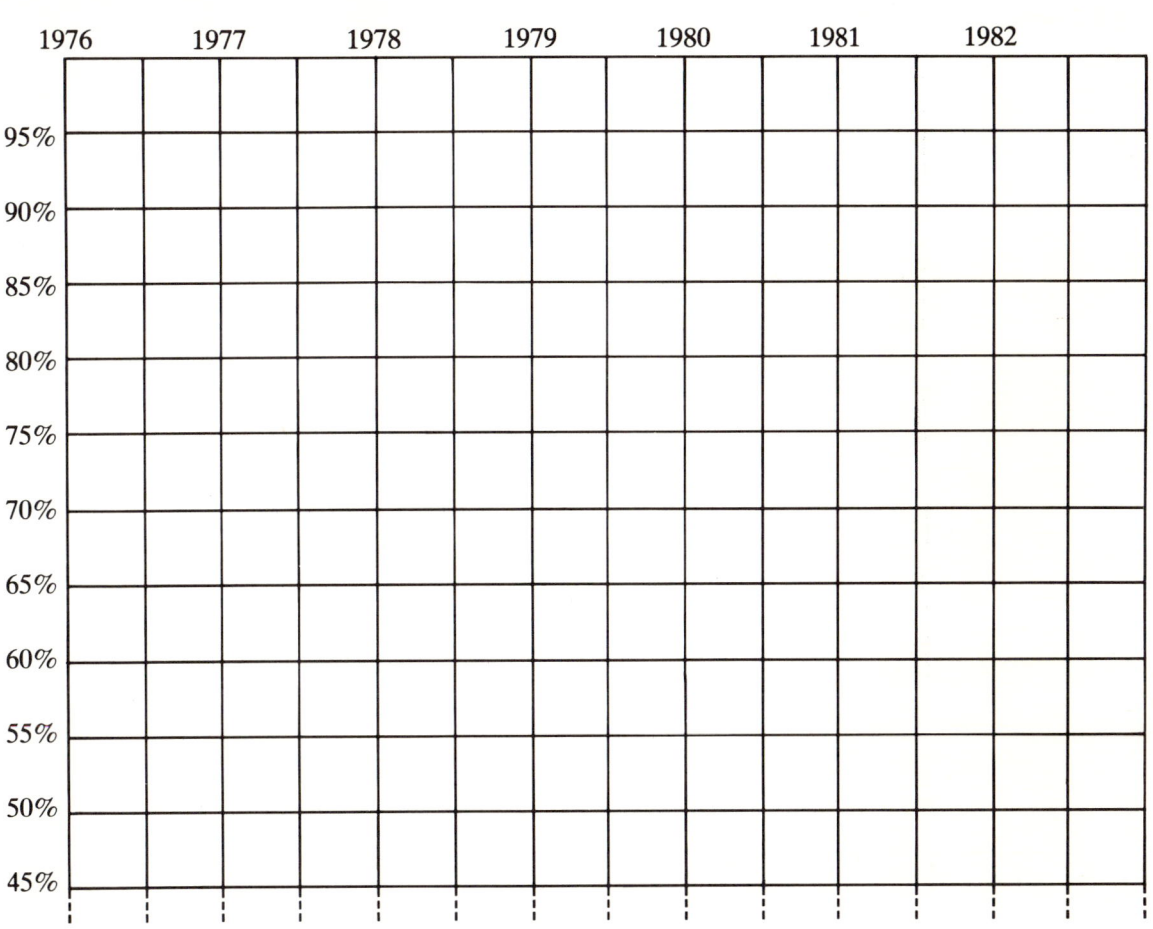

Appendix D Development and Testing of the Workbook

An accurate and simple method of financial self-analysis emerged from the process of developing the workbook. The steps outlined below trace that development.

Year One
1. Formed a working task force of experts in independent college financial assessment.
2. Identified through group consensus two small sets of prototypical colleges: one with few financial problems and one with many.
3. Through task force brainstorming, generated potential indicators that would separate the two types of schools.
4. Used data provided by John Minter Associates to test the indicators against the task force *a priori* assessments.
5. Redefined ambiguous indicators.
6. Visited four institutions to test the indicators against administrator perceptions.
7. Redefined and expanded indicators.
8. Visited four more institutions as in step 6.
9. Redefined and expanded indicators.
10. Published preliminary workbook.

Year Two
1. Used preliminary workbook as a training tool at four seminars, each attended by more than 20 administrators.
2. After seminar discussions, modified indicators.
3. Visited five additional institutions to test the workbook.
4. Modified workbook, expanding the analysis to strategic financial policy evaluation.
5. Rewrote text and expanded explanations of statistics.
6. In four different states held discussions, each attended by at least six schools that had used drafts of the workbook.
7. Modified and edited text.
8. Published final version.